PRAISE FOR

POSSESSING YOUR INHERITANCE

Learn to secure and obtain the inheritance God has planned for you as you read and study *Possessing Your Inheritance*. It will excite and ignite a vision for the destiny God has planned for you and for your future generations.

Elizabeth Alves
PRESIDENT, INTERCESSORS INTERNATIONAL
BULVERDE, TEXAS

Christians are supposed to walk in victory, but as the authors show, the only way we will inherit all that God has for us is to be in His will— to know His will for our lives and walk in it. Chuck D. Pierce writes prophetically to this "lost" generation to reveal the riches of obedience and the heart of God for His people.

Mike Bickle
MINISTRY DIRECTOR, FRIENDS OF THE BRIDEGROOM
SENIOR PASTOR, METRO CHRISTIAN FELLOWSHIP
KANSAS CITY, MISSOURI

As I read *Possessing Your Inheritance*, I was struck by two major themes. The first is "The Rest of God." My sense of seeing God as He is in the process of destroying and restoring the earth was heightened. The second, which is always in my heart, is "God's Covenant with His People." This everlasting covenant is meant to bring all those who have come to a saving knowledge of Christ into their eternal destiny. This is the first book I've read on this subject that has impacted me so deeply. The authors put it all into a fresh perspective to help the Body of Christ begin in a new way to possess their rightful inheritance.

Bobbye Byerly
DIRECTOR OF PRAYER AND INTERCESSION, WORLD PRAYER CENTER
COLORADO SPRINGS, COLORADO

PRAISE FOR

POSSESSING YOUR INHERITANCE

The great tragedy of the Church today is how few believers truly reach their Kingdom potential in Jesus. Finally, here is a practical and powerful plan to help us do just that, unveiled in one dynamic book.

Dick Eastman
INTERNATIONAL PRESIDENT, EVERY HOME FOR CHRIST
COLORADO SPRINGS, COLORADO

Make this profound principle of inheritance your own as this deep yet simple teaching engages you with a clear plan and a direction. Lay hold of what God has for you, your ministry and your church. Possessing our inheritance individually and corporately is critical to the Church in this hour.

Jane Hansen
PRESIDENT, AGLOW INTERNATIONAL
EDMONDS, WASHINGTON

Possessing Your Inheritance addresses a crucial topic for all followers of the Messiah—namely the importance of finding one's destiny in Him. This is central to our heritage. This very worthy book is practical, applicable, biblically sound, and clearly and simply written. I would desire that this book gain wide circulation. A pastor would be wise to see his members read this fine volume.

Daniel C. Juster
DIRECTOR, TIKKUN MINISTRIES
GAITHERSBURG, MARYLAND

PRAISE FOR
POSSESSING YOUR INHERITANCE

Chuck D. Pierce is a prophetic trumpet calling the Body of Christ into the victorious life Jesus promised. *Possessing Your Inheritance* is a clear sound for directing believers toward their God-given destiny!

Barbara Wentroble
BARBARA WENTROBLE MINISTRIES
DUNCANVILLE, TEXAS

POSSESSING YOUR INHERITANCE

POSSESSING
your
INHERITANCE

MOVING FORWARD IN
GOD'S COVENANT PLAN
FOR YOUR LIFE

Chuck D.
PIERCE & SYSTEMA
Rebecca Wagner

Renew

A Division of Gospel Light
Ventura, California, U.S.A.

Published by Renew Books
A Division of Gospel Light
Ventura, California, U.S.A.
Printed in U.S.A.

Renew Books is a ministry of Gospel Light, an evangelical Christian publisher dedicated to serving the local church. We believe God's vision for Gospel Light is to provide church leaders with biblical, user-friendly materials that will help them evangelize, disciple and minister to children, youth and families.

It is our prayer that this Renew book will help you discover biblical truth for your own life and help you meet the needs of others. May God richly bless you.

For a free catalog of resources from Renew Books/Gospel Light please contact your Christian supplier or contact us at 1-800-4-GOSPEL or at www.gospellight.com.

Cover Design by Kevin Keller
Interior Design by Rob Williams
Edited by Karen Kaufman

Library of Congress Cataloging-in-Publication Data
Pierce, Chuck D., 1953–
Possessing your inheritance / Chuck D. Pierce and Rebecca Wagner Sytsema.
     p.   cm.
Includes bibliographical references.
ISBN 0-8307-2357-9 (trade paper)
1. Christian life.   I. Sytsema, Rebecca Wagner.   II. Title.
   BV4501.2.P542   1999   98-56162
   248.4—dc21   CIP

2 3 4 5 6 7 8 9 10 11 12 13 14 15 / 05 04 03 02 01 00 99

Rights for publishing this book in other languages are contracted by Gospel Literature International (GLINT). GLINT also provides technical help for the adaptation, translation and publishing of Bible study resources and books in scores of languages worldwide. For further information, write to GLINT, P.O. Box 4060, Ontario, CA 91761-1003, U.S.A. You may also send E-mail to Glintint@aol.com, or visit their website at www.glint.org.

CONTENTS

FOREWORD

BY C. PETER WAGNER

When I first became a born-again Christian almost 50 years ago, I literally became a "new creature in Christ." Nothing in my up-bringing had prepared me for this. Other than being forced to attend Sunday School for a brief season in order for my parents to have some time alone on Sunday mornings, church and Jesus and prayer belonged in some other world. When I left home, I had no interest in God or religion, and my lifestyle, which embraced sin quite enthusiastically, gave no indication of what God might have in mind for me down the road.

Then things radically changed when my wife Doris came into my life and led me to the Lord as one of her prerequisites for agreeing to marry me. I woke up the next day with a new view of life and a new lifestyle from which I have never deviated. Before I became a Christian, however, I had a good mind. Whenever I graduated, I was always the valedictorian or the runner up. This carried over into my life as a Christian, and I was constantly trying to figure out exactly what this Christianity was that I had bought into.

Among other things, a book came out by John Stott called *Basic Christianity*. This was a remarkable book which, quite understandably, has exponentially outsold any book I have written. In it, John Stott was able to simplify what for many, including me, was a terribly complex matter—the Christian faith. *Basic Christianity* was an anointed book, used powerfully by the Holy Spirit to provide us with a fundamental understanding of why we believed what we did. As I read it, the fundamentals of the faith were spelled out so obviously that I found myself saying time after time, "Of course, why didn't I think of that long ago?"

I had exactly the same feeling when I first read this book, *Possessing Your Inheritance*. At this stage, I need no further explanation of the Christian religion. But I found myself marveling at insight after insight about the Christian life that I have been living for half a century. Chuck Pierce and Rebecca Sytsema have succeeded in simplifying numerous aspects of living for and serving God that I previously had chalked up as some of those theological mysteries that we will have to live with until we get to heaven. Their book could rightly be called "Basic Christian Living." Move over, John Stott!

My nature is not overly introspective. I am essentially a doer and an achiever. I have always heard respected people say, "God is not nearly as interested in what we do as He is in what we are." While I have never found adequate grounds to refute this contention, I must confess that I have always taken it with quite a generous grain of salt. Every time I have brought myself to read a book on the subject, I have become incurably bored after a chapter or two.

Until now! *Possessing Your Inheritance* is a book that cannot possibly bore any committed Christian who desires to be everything that God wants him or her to be. My generation regards Bill Bright's first spiritual law as just a degree or two under inspired Scripture: "God loves you and has a wonderful plan for your life." The other three spiritual laws have brought millions over the threshold of eternal life. The first part of God's "wonderful plan" is to be born again, but His plan for the rest of your life has never been more clearly spelled out than it is in this book.

Whether you have been a Christian for 5 months or 50 years, you will be blessed and enthralled by this anointed book. I can confidently say that, like *Basic Christianity*, *Possessing Your Inheritance* will exponentially outsell any book I have written! And it deserves to!

C. PETER WAGNER
Chancellor, Wagner Leadership Institute
Colorado Springs, Colorado

FOREWORD

BY CINDY JACOBS

Several years ago I prayed over Chuck Pierce at a prophetic conference held in Colorado Springs. The prayer became a prophecy that was catalytic to the theme of this book, *Possessing Your Inheritance*. In essence it said, "For I am going to deal with the dregs of those things which are holding you back from obtaining your full inheritance. I am going to restore the years the canker worm and locust have eaten in your life. Call back those things which have been stolen from your family." This was a revolutionary thought!

Later, my husband Mike, Chuck and I sat around pondering the meaning of this prophetic word. Could it be the Lord meant that Chuck would actually receive back the houses, land, large amount of finances, inheritance and potential for success that was lost to his family? While we didn't think he would have the exact same things restored, we felt that we were certainly on to something. We prayed and asked God to begin that day to completely restore his family.

The results were amazing! Though Chuck and his wife Pam had not owned a house for years, they have owned two since that time. Chuck's immediate and extended family were all reconciled to God, and the pain of the past has been replaced by great healing. What Chuck and Becky write about in this book really works! In fact, as Chuck reflected on his life, he began to understand how God had already begun this process of restoration over the years. However, when he intentionally began to believe God for the restoration of specific losses, the process went into an acceleration that was nothing short of incredible.

Although the stories in this book are about Chuck Pierce's life, Becky (or Rebecca as her name appears on the cover) has also lived these principles and seen them work in her own personal life. Becky was my secretary for four years—she is one brave, courageous lady. Not only is she a great writer, but she has lived through seeing her first little baby go to be with the Lord. Now Becky and her husband Jack have a beautiful son.

This book can change your life. If you apply the truths written in these pages, you too will experience the restoration of your generational inheritance. Inheritance that includes household salvation, prodigal sons returning, curses of poverty broken off of your family line, and health and blessing which will be passed on from generation to generation. You are in for an exciting journey with God.

Blessings!

CINDY JACOBS
Colorado Springs, Colorado
November 1998

ACKNOWLEDGMENTS

Not every book is a part of one's life. However, this book is a compilation of principals and wisdom resulting from defeats, woundings, healings, past victories and vision for the future. I liken myself to Paul when he exhorted the Philippians by saying, *"I also count all things loss for the excellence of the knowledge of Christ Jesus...that I may know Him and the power of His resurrection, and the fellowship of His sufferings, being conformed to His death...I know how to be abased, and I know how to abound. Everywhere and in all things I have learned both to be full and to be hungry, both to abound and to suffer need. I can do all things through Christ who strengthens me"* (Phil. 3:8,9; 4:13).

After the Lord began to teach me in His school of abasing and abounding, I then entered His course on possessing and securing. I am thankful to those who have helped me to know Christ. Being successful and accomplishing the very purpose of one's life requires much help from others. One definition of success is "to gain the available help along your road to reach your destination."

The Lord has placed many individuals along my "road" to help me accomplish His purpose in my life. The Church is advancing into a new day of leadership. Many are calling this leadership transformation the New Apostolic Reformation. One function of the apostolic leadership role in the Body is to "father and mother" a generation that is developing. I am thankful for those "fathers and mothers" who have supernaturally deposited and established the knowledge of the Living Lord Jesus Christ of Nazareth within me. From the time my earthly father died when I was 16, I have watched and recognized the leadership and influence the Lord has placed in my life.

Therefore, I want to honor Sid Cassidy, Alfred Croix, Ed Stephens, Billy J. Crosby, Jim Hylton, Ralph Mann and Jim Hodges for being fathers in the faith to me, and Robert Heidler for his teaching wisdom. I have also watched the Lord place godly, determined mothers in my life who have imparted great wisdom. I am thankful for my uncompromising grandmother, Inez LaGrone, now deceased, and my overcoming mother, Bernice L. Croix. I am very thankful for the mentoring of LaCelia Henderson and Bobbye Byerly in prayer. I am grateful to the Lord for placing Cindy Jacobs in my life to encourage me prophetically and to call forth gifts that I lacked confidence in using.

One of the joys of my life is to support visionaries. I am thankful for Peter and Doris Wagner and their incredible contribution to the history and direction of the Church. What a joy to colabor with them in the harvest fields and "build" with them the House of Prayer for all nations of the earth.

I could not have accomplished the writing of this book without my dear friend and coauthor Becky Wagner Sytsema. Not only can she communicate spiritual principles, but she has also walked out the principles of restoration in her own life. I dearly love Becky's husband Jack and thank him for being the "Martha" we needed to accomplish this project. I thank my two assistants, Brian Kooiman and June Rana, for keeping the "baggage in order" while I worked. Also, I thank my brother and sister, Keith and Penny Pierce, for allowing God to work in their lives to see the restoration of our family completed.

Most of all I want to acknowledge my wife Pamela. Because of her, I have gained revelation of the Glorious Bride. She is the model of my life. May her character of virtue be demonstrated in the Church that God is calling forth in the earth this hour.

My dear children Daniel, Rebekah, John Mark, Isaac and Ethan (and Joseph and Ron—children the Lord placed in our lives): Always remember to rise up and call your mother blessed and you will be blessed. Acknowledge her and you will secure your inheritance in the future.

Chuck D. Pierce

OUT OF THE RUINS

And they shall rebuild the old ruins, they shall raise up the former desolations, and they shall repair the ruined cities, the desolations of many generations.

—ISAIAH 61:4

Change! Conflict! Fear! Wars! Rumors of wars! Generations battling generations! Generations warring within themselves! The world is changing so quickly that many awaken with anxiety to each new day. I agree with Rick Joyner who says, "Change is now coming on the world so fast, that the only thing we can count on is change."[1]

How do we respond to all the changes around us? Do they overtake us? Are we a people being tossed to and fro with every societal, environmental and religious change that comes along?

Isaiah 33:6 says, *"Wisdom and knowledge will be the stability of your times"!* Stability means firmness of position; resistance to disintegration; not likely to fall; give way or overturn; firm or steady. Yet instead of stability, many Christians have seen change bring destruction to families, cites and nations. Change can bring fear.

But even in the face of earth-shattering change, God says, *Fear not! "But the people who know their God shall be strong, and carry out great exploits"* (Dan. 11:32). Carrying out great exploits means that we will take the available resources and cause multiplication to occur. Each of us has a future and a hope. In that future and hope, God has a plan for prosperity.

"Beloved, I pray that you may prosper in all things and be in health, just as your soul prospers" (3 John 2). My earnest desire is to help you achieve the goal summed up in this verse. God longs for you to prosper and succeed in life. He longs for you to accomplish all that He has destined for you to accomplish. And He longs to lead you down the road to possessing your inheritance. This book will help you understand keys to unlocking all that God intends for you so that you may truly prosper in all things.

POSITIONING FOR YOUR PORTION

One of the most beautiful stories about possessing inheritance comes from 2 Chronicles 20. In the context of this passage, a federation of enemy nations was coming against the tribe of Judah to overtake it. In days past, God had prevented Israel from invading these nations, because God always knows what wars can be won (see v. 7). He knew that as these enemy nations came together, their multiplied strength would overpower Judah.

Perhaps you can relate to this story, feeling as though numerous enemies are coming against you. It may seem that when you have defeated one, another rises. You may have seen many things in your life fall into rubble. But take heart! God is with you and He has a plan for overthrowing your enemies.

Such was the case in 2 Chronicles 20. Judah's king at the time was Jehoshaphat, who was a godly man. Through prayer and fasting,

Jehoshaphat sought the Lord for a strategy to defeat the enemies standing in the way of Judah's God-given inheritance (see v. 3). God is always faithful to those who cry out to Him. When Jehoshaphat cried out, God answered through a prophet who gave the following detailed instructions for victory:

1. They had to let go of fear. It was not their battle; it was God's (see v. 15).
2. They had to position themselves to meet the enemy head-on (see v. 17).
3. They were to stand still and see the salvation of God (see v. 17).
4. They had to believe by faith that God would defeat their enemies (see v. 20).
5. They had to believe the word of the prophets over their lives and inheritance (see v. 20).

As they followed God's plan, Jehoshaphat led them into worship and instructed the people to posture themselves in faith. Faith is that pause between knowing what God's plan is and seeing it actually take place. Faith sees the ruins. Faith sees what has been torn down. Faith sees what has never been completed. But faith can look at a situation and see what God sees—the thing already rebuilt or completed.

FAITH IS THAT PAUSE BETWEEN KNOWING WHAT GOD'S PLAN IS AND SEEING IT ACTUALLY TAKE PLACE.

So as they mingled their worship with faith, and obeyed God, the enemies who were set against them were utterly destroyed, and total victory was theirs (see v. 24). In fact, their enemies turned against each other and every one was killed. Not one had escaped (see v. 23).

As you read this book hopefully you, like Jehoshaphat, will cry out to God and find the keys for possessing your inheritance.

SUCCESS!

Jehoshaphat sought God and was successful in what he was to accomplish. God also longs for us to succeed—every one of us. He did not create us to be sad, defeated failures. Although that does not mean we will never *experience* failure, it does mean we are not created to *be* failures. Ponder, for a moment, the beautiful words of Psalm 139:17,18:

> *How precious also are Your thoughts to me, O God! How great is the sum of them! If I should count them, they would be more in number than the sand; when I awake, I am still with You.*

God's loving and precious thoughts were not only toward David, who wrote this Psalm, but they are also toward each and every one of us. Part of God's redemptive plan for our lives is to see that we gain whatever we need, whenever we need it, in order to accomplish His purposes for us. Those purposes include our success.

Success is defined as "turning out well or attaining a goal." It means to flourish, to prosper or to thrive. Success is God's will for our lives. Psalm 1:3 says the godly person *"shall be like a tree planted by the rivers of water, that brings forth its fruit in its season, whose leaf also shall not wither; and whatever he does shall prosper."* There is a portion, both spiritual and physical, that God has set aside for each of His children. As we learn what our portion is, and God moves us toward it, we become successful in our walk with Him.

Such was the case with Peter. When Jesus first laid eyes on Peter, He saw far more than a local fisherman; He saw a man with a high purpose in the kingdom of God. *"Then Andrew brought Simon to meet*

Jesus. Looking intently at Simon, Jesus said, 'You are Simon, the son of John— but you will be called Cephas [which means Peter]'" (John 1:42, *NLT*).

The name Peter means rock. Though Peter had his ups and downs while yet a disciple, and even denied Christ at the Crucifixion, it was after the Resurrection when the Lord said to Peter, *"And I also say to you that you are Peter, and on this rock I will build My church, and the gates of Hades shall not prevail against it"* (Matt. 16:18). And so it was that Peter became a great apostle, spreading the gospel and eventually giving his life for the cause of Christ.

Even though Peter was nothing particularly special at the time of their meeting, Jesus saw in him a great destiny. I suppose that Jesus knew a bumpy road would lie ahead for the young disciple. Even so, He set a course to lead and guide Peter through to the place where he would become a highly successful citizen of the kingdom of God, upon whom the Lord said He would build His Church.

Today, the Holy Spirit sees us just as Jesus saw Peter—reaching our fullest Kingdom potential. No matter where we are in life, or how insignificant we may feel, the Holy Spirit can see ahead to the day when we are successfully fulfilling the destiny for which we have been created. Just as Jesus called Peter by his new name long before its meaning became clear, so the Holy Spirit calls out to us in this hour—as children of destiny and success, even though we may seem far from it.

Specifically, the Lord longs for us to succeed:

- by moving our lives forward so we are not constantly living in the pain and regret of the past;
- by causing us to prevail over the enemy of our souls so that we are able to resist temptation and reclaim our inheritance;
- by causing us to act wisely and strategically;
- by promoting us to new levels at the right season; and
- by helping us to achieve our destined purposes when we cry out to Him along our paths.

In essence, as God's children, He longs for us to succeed even as He succeeds!

KEYS TO SUCCESS

Achieving the success and prosperity that God has for us is not automatic just because we are His children. We must cooperate and participate with the plan of God to help us move toward all He has for us. The following are some keys to help along the way:

1. Put God first. *"No one can serve two masters; for either he will hate the one and love the other, or else he will be loyal to the one and despise the other. You cannot serve God and mammon. Therefore I say to you, do not worry about your life, what you will eat or what you will drink; nor about your body, what you will put on. Is not life more than food and the body more than clothing?...For after all these things the Gentiles seek. For your heavenly Father knows that you need all these things.* **But seek first the kingdom of God and His righteousness, and all these things shall be added to you.** *Therefore do not worry about tomorrow, for tomorrow will worry about its own things"* (Matt. 6:24,25,32-34, emphasis added).

As this passage so clearly states, we cannot serve both God and the love of wealth. God is not merely a means to our financial security. People with that attitude will never reach their full potential until their hearts have been changed. God is not our servant. Instead, we are His servants. The apostle Paul, one of God's greatest success stories, wrote, *"I know how to be abased, and I know how to abound. Everywhere and in all things I have learned both to be full and to be hungry, both to abound and to suffer need. I can do all things through Christ who strengthens me"* (Phil. 4:12,13).

We may experience times of hunger in our lives, but if we are following God and seeking Him first, those times can be considered as a few pages in the book of our ultimate success. God knows what we need. The promise in Matthew 6 is that if we seek Him first, He will see to it that what we need, when we need it, will be there for us.

2. Follow covenant agreement. Every one of us who has experienced the saving grace of God has entered into a covenant agreement with Him. Many analogies are used throughout Scripture to define the relationship: He is our Father; we are His children. He is our Shepherd; we are the sheep of His pasture. He is the Head; we are the Body. He is the Master; we are the servants.

Each of these analogies paints a simple picture. It is up to God to provide for our needs, to promote us to the next level, to teach and guide us, to help us move forward and prevail. It is up to God to see that we have a portion and an inheritance. But, it is up to us to obey His commandments at every turn in order to see all His provision come to fruition. If we break the covenant through disobedience, rebellion, unbelief, sluggishness, forgetting God or hidden sin, we bring peril to our own success.

3. Seek strategy from God to reach your goal. The concept of reaching toward a goal is both wise and biblical. In Philippians 3, Paul writes, *"No, dear brothers and sisters, I am still not all I should be, but I am focusing all my energies on this one thing: Forgetting the past and looking forward to what lies ahead, I strain to reach the end of the race and receive the prize for which God, through Christ Jesus, is calling us up to heaven"* (vv. 13,14, *NLT*). Here Paul reveals that the success God has for us is not just for this earthly life, but will continue in heaven.

Reaching toward our goal of godly success seems to have a dual purpose. First, we are reaching toward our God-given potential to accomplish His plan for us while here on earth. Second, we are laying up a prize in heaven that is eternal. What a complete picture of success! God has a strategy for each of us to reach our goal. By seeking Him, we will gain pieces of the strategy along the way. As we are obedient to follow that strategy, we will one day stand before Him with confidence, knowing we reached the end of the race with success.

4. Live in Christ. *"For I live in eager expectation and hope that I will never do anything that causes me shame, but that I will always be bold for Christ, as I have been in the past, and that my life will always honor Christ, whether I live or I die. For to me, living is for Christ, and dying is even better"* (Phil. 1:20,21,

NLT). Here again, Paul brings success into an eternal perspective. To live for Christ and to honor Him in all that we do will bring us ultimate success and prosperity, whether we live or die. Many honorable saints throughout the history of the Church have shed their blood as martyrs for Christ Jesus. These are great success stories in the Kingdom.

But so, too, are those who live following Christ, not loving their lives unto death. These Christians are also honorable saints who are great success stories in the Kingdom. Success is as simple as knowing that when we allow Christ to lead us, we will always prosper in our souls, and that we will be blessed in all areas of life, both now and eternally.

Each one of us has a God-given destiny of success. That is a part of the inheritance we have as children of God. But what does having an inheritance in God really mean? Let's take a look.

WHAT IS INHERITANCE?

Webster describes inheritance as a portion, birthright or heritage; a right of ownership. As believers we must agree that the ultimate issue in inheritance is eternal life. There is no greater inheritance that we can ever hope to obtain. Once that issue is settled, the greatest portion of our eternal inheritance is secure.

But there is more to inheritance than a promise of everlasting life. In the Bible, inheritance is often used to describe the present or future blessings of the believer's spiritual life. Psalm 16:5, for instance, says, *"O Lord, You are the portion of my inheritance and my cup; you maintain my lot."* In the Sermon on the Mount, Jesus says, *"Blessed are the meek, for they shall inherit the earth"* (Matt. 5:5). Other such Scriptures include Acts 26:18: *"That they may receive forgiveness of sins and an inheritance among those who are sanctified by faith in Me,"* and Colossians 1:12: *"Giving thanks to the Father who has qualified us to be partakers of the inheritance of the saints in the light."*

As Christians, it is true that God has provided for us a rich spiritual inheritance, both here and in heaven, that no unbeliever will ever enjoy. Because our names are written in the Lamb's Book of Life, we have inherited such blessings as love, joy, peace and other fruit of the Spirit (see Gal. 5:22,23). As sons and daughters of righteousness, we have assurance of our heavenly standing. We know that God will never leave us or forsake us. The promises of inheritance for God's children are endless.

But figurative uses of inheritance, such as in the previously mentioned Scriptures, might lead us to believe that God's main interest in our inheritance is purely spiritual. Such Scriptures also seem to indicate that our inheritance is collective rather than individual. But God has a much more specific interest in each of us as individuals. Each of us has an inheritance that is uniquely our own. This unique inheritance includes many facets, such as our individual destinies, or that which God is longing to accomplish through each life for His glory.

It also includes physical inheritance, or those material things that God has set aside for each of us. Material possessions, such as money and lands, are important not only for our own necessity and enjoyment, but are also essential for the advancement of God's kingdom here on earth.

God's chosen spouse and our children may also be elements of personal inheritance. While they are part of our personal inheritance that we enjoy, they, specifically our children, are also recipients of our inheritance. Through our family, the deposit of God which He has placed in one generation can be passed on to the next generation and beyond. Proverbs 13:22 says, *"A good man leaves an inheritance to his children's children."* Possessing our inheritance is not just an issue for ourselves, but for our children and grandchildren.

So, what is inheritance? Simply this: Inheritance is possessing the portion that God has given you.

AN INHERITANCE NEVER POSSESSED

The catch is that many of us never take possession of our inheritance, at least in this lifetime. Take, for example, the fruit of the Spirit (see

Gal. 5:22,23). As Christians these qualities are available, even necessary, for each one of us. They are part of our inheritance. Nevertheless, many Christians do not have joy or peace and lack self-control in their lives. The fact is that these attributes rightfully belong to them, yet they have not been able to grasp what is theirs.

The reasons why believers have not possessed their inheritance are numerous. Often deep emotional hurts can cause a person to be so wounded that he or she has become immobilized. For example, I know a couple who experienced a miscarriage several years ago and became so paralyzed by the fear of losing another baby that they refuse to try again. The Lord may very well intend for this cou-

---

OFTEN POSSESSING OUR INHERITANCE MEANS JUST THAT—MOVING OUT AND ACTIVELY GRABBING HOLD OF WHAT THE LORD INTENDS TO BE OURS.

---

ple to have many children; however, their fear has immobilized them from cooperating with the inheritance the Lord has for them. This same kind of gripping fear is commonly evidenced among people who have been hurt in serious relationships and vowed never to venture out again. Fear becomes the stranglehold that cuts off their relational prosperity.

We need to understand that our inheritance is not necessarily an automatic part of our lives. Often possessing our inheritance means just that—moving out and actively grabbing hold of what the Lord intends to be ours. Consider the young couple fearful of pregnancy. By the mighty healing power of the Lord, they need to move away from fear of the unknown to trust in the Lord. Even though they may battle fear throughout a new pregnancy, *choosing* to trust in God's plan for them is the pathway to possessing their inheritance.

WHAT ABOUT THE SOVEREIGNTY OF GOD?

The thought that God has set aside an inheritance for us that we may never possess leads to an age-old question: What about the sovereignty of God? If He wants something to happen, isn't it a given? The answer is yes and no. Yes, God is indeed sovereign. He is the Author and Creator of our very existence, capable of intervening in any life at any given time.

Yet even the pages of Scripture tell of how the Lord, through an act of sovereignty, chose to give imperfect human beings dominion over the earth (see Gen. 1:28). Within the rules of that dominion, God gave to us the right to make our own choices and live with the consequences. We were given our own free will which, more often than not, seems to contradict God's will. As a result, God's perfect will has not necessarily been done on earth since the dawn of the human race. His will was clearly that Adam and Eve live in eternal communion with Him in the Garden of Eden. Yet they sinned. God's will was not done.

Another example is that the Lord is not willing that any should perish but that all should come to repentance (see 2 Pet. 3:9). Even so, people who have never come to repentance are perishing every minute of every day. God's will is not being done with each and every death of an unbeliever.

C. S. Lewis has this to say in his classic volume *Mere Christianity*:

God created things which had free will. That means creatures which can go either wrong or right. Some people think they can imagine a creature which was free but had no possibility of going wrong; I cannot. If a thing is free to be good, it is also free to be bad. And free will is what has made evil possible. Why, then, did God give them free will? Because free will, though it makes evil possible, is also the only thing that makes possible any love or goodness or joy worth having....Of course God knew what would happen if they used their freedom the wrong way: apparently He thought it worth the risk.[2]

The Lord's Prayer itself offers further proof that God's will is not apparently an automatic occurrence, at least here on earth. Jesus taught the disciples to pray that God's kingdom would come and His will would be done on earth as it is in heaven (see Matt. 6:10; Luke 11:2). Apparently, the will of God is not an issue in heaven, yet it is here on earth. If that were not so, this prayer would be a redundant, powerless ritual. In fact, all prayer outside of that which refreshes our relationship to God would be useless.

Dutch Sheets, pastor of Springs Harvest Fellowship in Colorado Springs, Colorado, recently wrote a brilliant book entitled *Intercessory Prayer* in which he has the following to say on the issue of God's will:

> Without question, *humans were forever to be God's link to authority and activity on the earth.*
>
> Here we have, I believe, the reason for the necessity of prayer. God chose, from the time of the Creation, to work on the earth through humans, not independent of them. He always has and always will, even at the cost of becoming one. Though God is sovereign and all-powerful, Scripture clearly tells us that He limited Himself, concerning the affairs of earth, to working through human beings.[3]

Earlier in Sheets's book, he quotes E. M. Bounds:

> God shapes the world by prayer. The more praying there is in the world, the better the world will be, the mightier the forces against evil....The prayers of God's saints are the capital stock of heaven by which God carries on His great work upon earth. God conditions the very life and prosperity of His cause on prayer.[4]

So what does this mean to us in terms of inheritance? Simply this: Even as Adam lost his God-intended inheritance in the Garden of Eden, we too, through sin and disobedience, are vulnerable to the same potential. However, we also serve a faithful, merciful God who had a plan for restoration of what was lost. Through Jesus, God restored to the human race that which was lost through Adam. God has the same desire in our own lives. Even if you have lost inheritance, God has a plan to restore it to you.

"I WILL RESTORE TO YOU ALL THAT YOU HAVE LOST"

The story of my own life has been a prophetic picture of restoration. God has been faithful to restore inheritance lost in my own family's history through turbulent, abusive years.

A FAMILY ESTABLISHED

As a child, I do remember some happy years. Even at a young age I recognized that there was a purpose in the family unit, and I somehow knew God had a plan for our family. During those happy years, our family was being established. My father was a hard working, creative person who had great potential for prosperity. Not only was he successful at the company he worked for, but he also made a good business of horses, cattle and property. His family owned acres of beautiful land in East Texas. His father came from a family of 12 children. As that generation began to die, my dad began to buy the land from his aunts and uncles. Eventually we built a beautiful home where the original family home had been, high on a hill overlooking a lake. It was a vivid picture of our family living in the fullness of our inheritance.

During that time, I was unknowingly learning a great deal about the importance of the family unit in God's eyes. The Bible is full of genealogies and family stories. The family many biblical characters belonged to determined both their rightful place in life and their inheritance. God deals with families in the same way He deals with individuals. All the same principles of sowing and reaping, and blessing and cursing apply.

Furthermore, the family unit is meant to be a prophetic picture of the family of God. In her book *What Is a Family?*, Edith Schaeffer says, "A family—parents and grandparents and children, the larger combination of three or four generations, or one little two-generation family—is meant to be a picture of what God is to His Family."[5] God's plan for the family is a place of love, peace, security, discipline and so on—many of the same things we can experience in the family of God. The family unit is also a great conduit of inheritance being passed from one generation to the next, and is meant to be a blessing to the world through the proper use of that inheritance.

A FAMILY DESTROYED

However, the enemy knows the power of the family unit and hates it with a passion. Satan has strategies to tear apart whatever God longs to establish. So, even though God's plan for the family may be a picture of Himself, many families lie in tattered shreds leaving devastated lives in their wake. Such was the case in my family. Everything that had been built, the enemy had a plan to destroy.

Over a period of time, my father began to fall into alcoholism and became emotionally and physically abusive to the rest of us. As he spiraled downward, Dad became involved in prostitution, gambling and various other means of corruption. The constant violence in our home was destroying the family. Our family unit, which once had great potential to thrive, began to degenerate and became a breeding ground for brokenness. What I had known and cherished in my heart as a young child no longer existed. This deplorable lifestyle went on for 10 memorable years.

Even though my mother was a godly woman, she was caught up in the turmoil of our home. All Mom could do was try to protect us and somehow keep us from falling completely apart. She knew in her heart that the Lord could deliver my father, but she did not know how to battle the enemy's power which had so thoroughly blinded my father's spiritual, emotional and physical eyes.

I had been truly saved when I was 11, but the turmoil at home prevented me from developing a real foundation in God. I would go to Sunday School and learn Scriptures, but I still did not have an intimate relationship with the Lord. Even though I would pray and cry out for deliverance, my family was in such constant trauma that I simply could not find any peace. Finally, when I was 16, my father died a sudden, premature death. When Dad died, I knew that even though death was not God's perfect will for his life, all things would work together for good and that this was God's way of saving what remained of our lives. From our secure family, to our land and our home, we had lost everything during those terrible years.

For about a year after my father's death, I sincerely followed after the Lord. But then a strange thing happened. The rejection, shame and abandonment I had experienced caused me to hide from God. And because I lacked an intimate relationship with Him, I began to turn from the road that God had paved for me to follow, a path that would have eventually led me into the same things that had destroyed my dad. Romans 7:15,18,19 says, *"I do not understand what I do. For what I want to do I do not do, but what I hate I do....I know that nothing good lives in me, that is, in my sinful nature. For I have the desire to do what is good, but I cannot carry it out. For what I do is not the good I want to do; no, the evil I do not want to do—this I keep on doing"* (NIV).

These verses were indeed working themselves out in my life. I hated what I was doing, yet I still followed the wrong path. I knew that I had great potential and that, even though my family had suffered many hard years, I still had a lot going for me. I did not want to lose the potential. Deep within my heart I somehow knew that despite all the trouble we had been through as a family, God had a plan to bring restoration.

A GODLY INFLUENCE

Even in the midst of my rebellion, I did have a godly influence through my maternal grandmother—a wonderful, strong lady who always said what she thought. Grandma lived in a way that acknowledged the Lord in her own life and in the lives of those around her. In fact, if my father had respect for anyone during his time of turmoil, it was my mother's mother. I too respected her greatly and enjoyed spending time with her.

One day during my period of rebellion, I went to my grandmother's house for lunch. As we visited, Grandma began to express her concern for me. She could see that I was pursuing the same path that led my father to destruction and that I would suffer the same fate if I did not turn to the Lord. Though I loved and respected her, I flatly announced that I was not interested in hearing what she had to say about my lifestyle.

Now my grandmother always had a way of getting your attention when she felt you were not listening. On that day she calmly set my lunch down on the table, and without any warning, slapped me hard across the face with the back of her hand. She was serious! As I reeled from the blow, Grandma assured me that she would not bring it up again, but that she would allow the Lord to deal with me according to the call He had on my life. I had no idea what she meant. But thank God for godly grandmothers! Their prayers store up an inheritance to be released as we begin to follow after God.

OUT OF THE RUINS

Three months later I found myself in a hospital room—I was a physical wreck. Working, going to college and leading a fairly avid night life had taken a toll on my body. I had finally collapsed from exhaustion and double pneumonia. It so happened that my grandmother was a nurse in that same hospital. She couldn't help but remind me that something like this was bound to happen.

In God's mercy, I shared the hospital room with a Pentecostal preacher who spoke to me for days about the grace of God. The principles he shared suddenly began to make sense. I knew in my spirit that what he was saying was right. After he was released from the hospital, I began reading the Bible as never before. I also read *The Cross and the Switchblade* (Chosen Books), David Wilkerson's classic tale of God's redemption in the life of vicious gang member Nicky Cruz. That book spoke to me of God's grace and mercy.

Six days into my stay in the hospital, something absolutely supernatural began to happen. I can only describe it as a beautiful presence of the Lord—a visitation from God. For three days I wept over the many things that had happened in my life. Until then, I had never released my emotions so they could begin to be healed.

Those days brought a tremendous cleansing to both my heart and my spirit. At one point, God's presence entered the room, and He spoke to me in a voice so loud it seemed audible: "I will restore all that you have lost." With those words, He penetrated every part of my being. Though I had suspected it before, I now knew that God had a plan not only to go back and heal the wounds of our past, but also to restore my future, my godly inheritance.

In fact, one day as I was driving to work, I felt the presence of the Lord overwhelm me. I pulled the car over, and the Lord began to show me how much He loved me and just how much He had truly loved my father. I saw how Satan had gained entrance in my father's life. Then I realized that as Dad had given in to various temptations, he had come into agreement with the enemy's plan for him rather than God's plan. The result of that process was his premature death. But, because of God's love for my father, He poured the inheritance that should have been Dad's onto me. As God showed me this, my victim mentality melted away. I saw that my father was not the enemy, but that a real enemy had come in and swept my father onto a destructive path. I began to have a true love and compassion toward my dad.

Much later in my life, a Sunday School teacher explained that I had both an evil inheritance and a godly inheritance, and I had chosen the godly. I shudder to imagine what my life would have been like had I chosen to follow after the evil inheritance left by my father. I thank God that He arrested me in my tracks and, through His merciful grace and the backhand of my grandmother, so clearly led me toward His plan for me. I have followed the Lord with all my heart, and I have indeed watched Him keep His promise to bring restoration to many, many areas of my life.

WHAT IS RESTORATION?

As sons and daughters of Adam, we have been in desperate need of restoration since the Garden of Eden. So much of what God intended for us, our original inheritance at the time of creation, was lost through sin and replaced with evil fruit. Where human beings once enjoyed intimate fellowship with God, they were now faced with a wall of separation that was humanly impossible to penetrate. Innocence gave way to self-consciousness and sin. Eternal life in communion with God was replaced by death in judgment. So much lost! But God truly is a God of restoration, and He has a plan for the restoration of the human race. Through His Son, we are now able to return to intimate fellowship with God, renewed innocence and the promise of eternal life. Restoration is the very nature of God.

Acts 3:19-21 says, *"Repent therefore and be converted, that your sins may be blotted out, so that times of refreshing may come from the presence of the Lord, and that He may send Jesus Christ, who was preached to you before, whom heaven must receive until the times of restoration of all things, which God has spoken by the mouth of all His holy prophets since the world began."* The moment Adam sinned, God set the process of restoration in motion. Throughout the ages He spoke to His prophets about this holy reversal. Some of these prophecies have been fulfilled. Others, including the second coming of Christ, will be fulfilled in the future. We are in the midst of seeing the greatest plan of restoration the world will ever know unfold right before us!

The simple truth is that *God is more interested in restoration than in judgment!* Even in His judgment, God has a plan to restore. God used Noah, for example, as an instrument of restoring and replenishing the earth after harsh judgment. Later, we see time and time again how God judged the nation of Israel for its wickedness and disobedience. Yet each time, God restored Israel to Himself. God's nature and purpose in an individual's life is no different. Judgment is reaping what we have sown and will often bring areas of desolation or fruitlessness in our lives. Even though we are forgiven through the blood of Jesus, there may still be consequences to pay. Though we may experience judgment for what we or those in generations before us have done, be assured that somewhere in all our suffering, God has a plan to bring restoration and to get us back on course so that we might receive our inheritance and fulfill our intended destinies.

To restore means to revive and return to life, or to bring back to a former or original condition. This definition, however, falls short of all that restoration in God means. God intends to do more than bring us back to a former or original condition. He intends to multiply and increase us beyond that point. He longs for our latter days to be greater than our former days. God's plan for *you* is restoration!

LIFE MORE ABUNDANT

What is it, then, that God is longing to restore to us? Simply put, He wants to restore life—the life that He destined for us. His primary method of restoration is through the redemptive work of Jesus. In order for us to have an adequate understanding of what life in Jesus means, let's take a look at a familiar passage. In John 10:10 Jesus says, *"I have come that they may have life, and that they may have it more abundantly."* This verse is full of tremendous promises and certainly bears the need for a closer look.

First, this passage promises "that they might have." The "they" referred to in this passage becomes clear as we read the context. Jesus is speaking of Himself as the Good Shepherd and "they" are the sheep of His pasture. This passage, therefore, is written to include every one of us who are His sheep. If you have accepted Jesus as your Savior and follow Him as your Lord, the promises of this passage are for you.

"Might have" is a key phrase to the concept of possession. We will delve into the whole issue of possessing in some detail in chapter 9, but for now let's take a look at it here in this passage. From the Greek word *echo*, "might have" includes the idea of having or holding in one's hand, or in the sense of wearing as a piece of clothing. Included in the meaning is to own or possess external things such as property or riches; to be joined by the bonds of natural blood, marriage, friendship, duty or law; to lay hold of a thing, to adhere or cling to; to be closely joined to a person or thing.[6] The life that Jesus promises to bring is meant to be our possession—so much a part of us that it is bound to us and we to it.

So, what exactly is life? Physically, life is the property in animals, plants and humans that makes it possible for them to obtain supply which will produce energy, create growth, adapt themselves to their surroundings and reproduce their kind. Though this may be a strict definition of life, Jesus is talking about much more than simply having existence and reproducing. The Greek word *zoe* is what has been translated in this passage as life. *Zoe* means to be possessed of vitality; to have life active and vigorous; to be devoted to God; to be blessed; to be among the living (not lifeless, not dead); to enjoy real life, true life worthy of the name; to pass life on to others; to be fresh, strong, efficient, active, powerful; to be endless in the kingdom of God.[7] From this definition Jesus is clearly referring to physical life and spiritual life rich in quality and quantity, since this word also denotes eternal life in the kingdom of God.

But Jesus does not stop there. Not only are we to enjoy such a quality of life and a future hope of eternity, we are also to have it "more abundantly." *Perissos*, the Greek word for abundantly, means excessive, overflowing, surplus, over and above, more than enough, profuse, extraordinary, more than sufficient, superior, more remarkable, more excellent.[8]

In summary, God's intentions for us are truly amazing. He longs to take us from a place of judgment, desolation and fruitlessness to a place of abundant restoration and increase of life!

Notes

1. Rick Joyner, *The Surpassing Greatness of His Power* (Charlotte, N.C.: Morningstar Publications, 1996), p. 9.
2. C. S. Lewis, *Mere Christianity* (New York, N.Y.: Macmillan Publishing Co., Inc., 1943), p. 52.
3. Dutch Sheets, *Intercessory Prayer* (Ventura, Calif.: Regal Books, 1996), pp. 28-29.
4. Ibid., pp. 23-24.
5. Edith Schaeffer, *What Is a Family?* (Grand Rapids, Mich.: Baker Book House, 1975), p. 45.
6. James Strong, *The New Strong's Exhaustive Concordance of the Bible* (Nashville, Tenn.: Thomas Nelson Publishers, 1990), ref. 2192.
7. Ibid, ref. 2198 and 2222.
8. Ibid, ref. 4053.

T W O

THE PROCESS OF
RESTORATION

He has delivered us from the power of darkness and conveyed
us into the kingdom of the Son of His love, in whom we have
redemption through His blood, the forgiveness of sins.

—COLOSSIANS 1:13,14

We have looked at "what" God wants to restore to us, which is *zoe*
life. Now let's look at the two basic "how" elements in the process
of restoration. The first, which is the starting point of all restoration, is understanding and coming into salvation. The second is
understanding and coming into wholeness.

UNDERSTANDING SALVATION

Restoration begins with knowing what salvation is and what it does
for us. Many people have a narrow view of salvation. They see it as a

way to escape from the deadly consequences of sin, and they view repentance as a striving toward moral purity. Therefore, they believe that if we ask Jesus to save us and we in turn live good, clean lives, we have a ticket to heaven. This view not only leads to a distorted and somewhat legalistic relationship with God and each other, but it also totally negates the overall joy and true benefits of salvation.

Salvation comes from the Greek word *soterion*, meaning to rescue, deliver, bring to safety, liberate, release or cause preservation. The word is linked to the concepts of forgiveness, healing, prosperity and restoration. All of these benefits are implied within the word that gives Christians their greatest hope and joy.

Without salvation, there is no restoration! There is no hope for getting back on the track God intended for us, both collectively and as individuals, from the foundation of the earth. God has an intended destiny for every human being. The first step to entering into that destiny is salvation through Jesus Christ—not just saying the Sinner's Prayer and letting it go at that, but allowing the forgiveness, healing, prosperity and restoration to penetrate every part of our lives.

Upon seeing the baby Jesus, Simeon declared, *"For my eyes have seen Your salvation which You have prepared before the face of all peoples, a light to bring revelation to the Gentiles, and the glory of Your people Israel"* (Luke 2:30-32). Simeon saw Jesus and recognized the salvation of the Lord. Yet imagine how many of his contemporaries saw the same child, the same young man, and never recognized salvation in their midst.

Those who do recognize the necessity for true, life-changing salvation have tapped into the only true source of restoration, the only true source of life this world has to offer. Through salvation in Jesus Christ, we are not only restored to the Father (although that in itself would surely be enough), but we are also forgiven, healed and brought into our prosperity. What a hope and a future we have!

UNDERSTANDING WHOLENESS

Salvation permeates our entire being—body, soul and spirit—with the ability to change every fiber of our makeup. As we yield to the ongoing, life-changing power of salvation, we can begin to understand wholeness.

When we came to the Lord, no matter what age we were, we were all fragmented with pieces of our lives scattered here and there. Why? Because scattering is a curse that we come under as a result of sin. When we sin, pieces of the person God intends for us to be are left behind. We trade purity, blessing, health, and/or a part of God's perfect plan for our lives for a sin we have committed. Therefore, parts of the whole person God intends for us to be lie scattered along the paths of our lives at each point where we have chosen sin.

Although we in the Western world tend to compartmentalize our lives into physical, mental and spiritual (or body, soul and spirit), the fact is that a proper biblical worldview is one of a unified, whole person in whom these parts are not separate entities, but are interconnected. First Thessalonians 5:23 says, *"Now may the God of peace Himself sanctify you completely; and may your whole spirit, soul, and body be preserved blameless at the coming of our Lord Jesus."* Here we see that God's interest in sanctifying is not limited to the spiritual being of a person, but the whole person. The concept of dealing with a person holistically did not originate in the Far East or in New Age thinking; it originated with God.

In fact, Jesus' message was one of wholeness. Many times He would respond to those whom He touched by saying, "Your faith has made you whole." Why? As previously mentioned, sin can leave us scattered. Sin also affects each part of us. Sin is not just a dark blot on the invisible realm of the soul; it can affect us physically, mentally, emotionally or spiritually. Many people are facing illnesses today because of sin in their lives. For this reason, we must transcend our Western mind-set and realize that we need restoration and wholeness to be brought to every part of our being.

E. Anthony Allen, in the book *Transforming Health* edited by Eric Ram, states:

> The ways people think, feel, relate and manage their life-styles can maim and even kill. But divine healing and renewed hope can transcend normal healing processes. Divine forgiveness, reconciliation, deliverance, restoration and renewal bring healing. Where God reigns there is healing. Wholeness comes not by "treating" but by healing.[1]

That is why Jesus said, "Your faith has made you whole." When He heals, He restores, and restoration is a holistic process. Only God has the power to gather the scattered pieces of our sin-ridden lives and bring them back into wholeness.

That is part of what happened to me when I was 18. When the Lord said, "I will restore to you all that you have lost," I entered into a process of exchanging my earthly, fragmented life for a wholeness that gave me the power to obtain all the spiritual blessings that God had stored up for me in heavenly places. My body, soul and spirit all entered into that process. Throughout this book, I will share different areas of my life that the Lord has faithfully and miraculously restored to me. I am, however, still in this process—we all are. Since age 18, I have faced other losses in my life that need restoration. But God has always been more than faithful to meet my every need!

THE HOLY SPIRIT: OUR AGENT OF RESTORATION

We've talked about the "what" and "how" of restoration. Now let's look at the "who." The Holy Spirit is the person of the Godhead who is serving as the restorative agent here on earth. God the Father is the author of our restoration plan. He manifested Himself on earth through His son, Jesus. Jesus carried within Him that plan and, consequently, our future. He took the sin that would stop our personal future and let it be crucified on the Cross with Him. This act insured our restoration and future success.

Jesus then said to His disciples, *"Nevertheless I tell you the truth. It is to your advantage that I go away; for if I do not go away, the Helper will not come to you; but if I depart, I will send Him to you....All things that the Father has are Mine. Therefore I said that He will take of Mine and declare it to you"* (John 16:7,15).

WHO IS THE HOLY SPIRIT?

The Holy Spirit has an essential role in the life of every believer, with a vast job description. Some Christians only associate the filling of the Holy Spirit with those things that are considered "charismatic," such as tongues, and therefore prefer to ignore His function. They limit themselves to a very narrow view of the One whom Jesus called our Helper. The word "helper" in Greek is *parakletos*, meaning intercessor, counselor, advocate or comforter. What a beautiful promise of a constant help.

But that's not all. In his book *The Names of the Holy Spirit*, vice president of Liberty University Elmer Towns expounds on a list of 126 descriptive names, titles and emblems of the Holy Spirit found in Scripture. These references to the Holy Spirit include Breath of Life (Rev. 11:11); a Dove (Mark 1:10); the Finger of God (Luke 11:20); the Guarantee of Our Inheritance (Eph. 1:14; cf. 2 Cor. 5:5); the Oil of Gladness (Ps. 45:7; Heb. 1:9); Rivers of Living Water (John 7:38); The Spirit of...Promise (Eph. 1:13); Adoption (Rom. 8:15); Counsel (Isa. 11:2); the Fear of the Lord (Isa. 11:2); Glory (1 Pet. 4:14); Grace (Zech. 12:10; Heb. 10:29); Holiness (Rom. 1:4); Judgment (Isa. 4:4); Knowledge (Isa. 11:2); Life (Rom. 8:2); Love (2 Tim. 1:7); Might (Isa. 11:2); Power (2 Tim. 1:7); Prophecy (Rev. 19:10); Revelation (Eph. 1:17); a Sound Mind (2 Tim. 1:7); Supplication (Zech. 12:10); Truth (John 14:17); Understanding (Isa. 11:2); and Wisdom (Exod. 28:3; Deut. 34:9).[2]

Only when we allow the Holy Spirit to work within us do we have the power to live a victorious Christian life. And it is He, the Holy Spirit, who does the work of restoring the fragmented, scattered pieces of our lives to something that is far greater than its former state. When we receive the Holy Spirit's work in our lives, and yield to His direction, we have access to all that the Father desires for us. The restoration process can begin.

THE NEW WINESKIN

When the Holy Spirit begins a process of restoration, He has placed us in a new season with new revelation and new life: a new wine. Most of us are familiar with the passage in Matthew 9:17 that says, *"Nor do they put new wine into old wineskins, or else the wineskins break, the wine is spilled, and the wineskins are ruined. But they put new wine into new wineskins, and both are preserved."*

In order to contain the new wine of restoration, we need a new wineskin. The Greek word for new, meaning something totally new that has never been seen before, is *neos*. But that's not the word used in this passage. The word used in this passage is *kainos*, meaning something that has been renewed or made over—something restored.

TO MAKE A WINESKIN NEW, HE SOAKS AN OLD WINESKIN IN WATER AND RUBS IT IN OIL. HARD THINGS WE GO THROUGH ARE THE OIL THAT HE RUBS INTO US. BUT THAT OIL ALSO CONTAINS A NEW ANOINTING.

In the restorative process, God takes what was there and brings it to a new place so He can pour within it that which He longs to release to us—our new wine. To make a wineskin new, He soaks an old wineskin in water and rubs it in oil. Rubbing in the oil is the part of the process that makes us flexible. Those hard things we go through are the oil that He rubs into us. And that oil also contains a new anointing. As we allow the Holy Spirit to take us through the process of rubbing, we not only become more flexible so that we can handle all God desires to pour into us, but we also become able to pour out in a greater measure.

THREE THINGS REMOVED

So, how does the wineskin change? How do we become renewed so we can begin to move forward in our restoration? First, a process of removal must occur. Specifically, there are three things that God must remove from our lives in order to renew our wineskins.

1. He removes legalism. Most Christians would be greatly surprised to learn how many legalistic structures they have embraced. Simply put, legalism is narrowing all of our mind processes down to the point that we can't receive the mind of God. Rather than having a mind-set that is saturated in His grace and love, legalism is a mind-set that is steeped in man's judgment and control. Legalism always leads to pride and unbelief. In Galatians, legalism is even equated with witchcraft. Paul reminds the Galatians that they were doing great. They were having a good time, growing in the Lord and walking in faith. Then he asks who has bewitched them? In other words, who narrowed their minds down to such a degree that they were no longer able to receive the grace of God? Who brought legalism into their midst?

Our restoration cannot be released while God is tightly locked in a box. We must allow the Lord to remove our legalistic, religiously rigid mind-sets. For example, is there a situation in your life, in your family or in your city that seems completely unchangeable? Are behavioral patterns so deeply entrenched that nothing could shake them loose? If the answer is yes, then you are dealing with a legalistic mind-set. We *say* nothing is impossible with God, but do we really *believe* nothing is impossible with God? In every area where we do not have this heartfelt assurance, we have a legalistic, bewitching structure that narrows God. Ask the Lord to reveal hidden places of legalism in your mind, and then be willing to let those old structures fall to the ground. Allow new faith to rise up within you. This is a key to becoming flexible wineskins.

2. He removes condemnation. Satan is a liar and a thief. He lies to us about our position with God in order to steal the restoration God has for us. One of his favorite tactics is to bombard believers with reminders of personal failures or failures in their generations to the point where they wear around a sticky garment of condemnation and guilt. They say things such as, "God can't restore me because I...am divorced, had an abortion, had an affair, lied about a friend, took what was not mine (fill in the blank)."

These are lies! You don't have to wear that old garment. The cycle of the past can end. Getting right with God and then forgiving yourself will break the schemes the devil intended to use to keep you draped in a shroud of guilt, no matter what you've done. Jack Hayford writes, "And once your relationship with God is restored, your guilt has served its purpose and no longer has any place in your life. Let it go. And refuse its argument to regain any place in tormenting your mind or your feelings."[3]

Let the Holy Spirit soak you in His cleansing waters of forgiveness and renewal. This is another key to renewing the wineskin that will hold the wine of restoration.

3. He removes judgmentalism. Just as we must put away our own condemnation, so must we put away condemning others through judgmentalism. Because of the law of sowing and reaping, we really can't fully do one without the other. If we condemn others, we will be condemned. And what's worse, the Bible says that we too become dangerously susceptible to falling into the *same* sin we accuse others of. Don't be fooled. We are not to sit in judgment. Judgmentalism has serious spiritual ramifications and has the power to keep us from entering into restoration.

Isaiah 58 says that if you will pray and fast, and let God determine the fast for you (don't do it religiously), and if you'll *put away the pointing of that finger and looking outward*, He will begin to break forth your light and your healing will spring up. Allow that process of God to bring you into the fullness He has for you. This, too, is part of making the wineskin clean and ready for the new wine.

THREE THINGS RESTORED

In the process of renewing our wineskins, certain things must be restored to us in order to make the process complete. Here are three key factors that move us toward restoration:

1. He restores intimate contact with Himself and others. Relationship is difficult for many Christians simply because our society breeds fear of intimacy. We protect ourselves. We don't want to get hurt. We don't want to allow our emotions to be seen. And to complicate matters, those who have experienced broken relationships in the past don't want to chance future intimacy. But the simple fact is that we need one another. We need God. Without one or the other, we will never enter into the fullness of restoration. We must begin to allow God to make us intimate communicators with Himself and then each other.

First and foremost, we need to embrace an intimate relationship with God. The classic analogy is Mary and Martha (see Luke 10:38-42). We get so caught up in what we are to do that we forget what we are about. Mary sat at the feet of Jesus until she knew her destiny. Once she knew the purpose of her life, then she could go do the dishes with Martha, or anything else that needed to be done. She did not neglect the task. Through intimacy, Mary simply gained what she needed for her life and then tended to the business of the house. God is calling us into a new intimate place. From this intimate place, we gain our new strategies for moving ahead.

But the intimacy is not for ourselves alone. Just as God wants to restore us as individuals, He is equally interested in restoring us as the Bride of Christ. For that reason, we must allow Him to bring us into intimate relationships with one another that will thrust us forward into our biblical destiny.

2. He begins to restore our Father/child relationship. When we do not know God as Abba Father and have not yet come into the spirit of adoption that God has for us, we really do not have the relationship needed to grasp our restoration and the inheritance that comes with it. This is important to understand. Many times God starts by dealing with our earthly father and authority issues in order to restore the Father/child relationship that we have with Him. In cases where our fathers have abused their authority, or did not take their proper role in the family, God must restructure our thinking, but we must let Him. He is neither an abusive Father nor an absent Father. He is a loving Father who cares deeply for us—so much so that He has a plan of restoration for our lives. We need to allow Him to bring us to that understanding. Once those issues are in order, the word of the Lord over our lives can begin to spring forth.

3. God restores our childlike faith. God sees all the war and wilderness places that we have been in. Through those times, He begins to increase our measure of faith. As this childlike faith begins to arise, the glory of God rests upon us.

I have always considered myself a man of faith. I lead meetings all around the world filled with great faith and expectation of what God will do. Nonetheless, I learned a new lesson about childlike faith recently. In addition to many other responsibilities, I had just begun working with C. Peter Wagner, Doris Wagner and Ted Haggard in a project called the World Prayer Center (WPC). This unique project holds great potential for raising up massive amounts of prayer throughout the world. It also holds equal potential as a target for spiritual warfare.

My job as executive director of the WPC included leading the intercession needed for raising the necessary funds to support the project. Because of the level of warfare we had experienced, I knew that I did not have the faith I needed for seeing the project through. One morning I asked the Lord to increase my measure of faith concerning the WPC. That same day I was on my way down to South Texas to lead a revival meeting. While I was preparing to leave, my 15-year-old son Daniel came to me and said, "Daddy, when you're in South Texas, I believe God wants you to bring me back a parrot."

Chuckling at him, I replied, "Daniel, parrots cost $1,500. Why don't you go ask the Lord if He really wants you to have a parrot? If He does, He'll get one for you."

Accepting my statement, Daniel darted out of the room. About 10 minutes later, he returned and flatly declared, "Daddy, I asked the Lord about my parrot, and He said He wants me to have one."

I could not believe it. What could I say? I left, shaking my head and wondering if I had somehow taught him to manipulate what he was hearing from God.

When I arrived in South Texas, I told the couple I was staying with about my conversation with Daniel. The man and I just laughed it off. But the wife looked at me and said, "Parrots fly over the border from Mexico through here all the time." I looked at her and wondered what that had to do with anything. We could never catch a wild parrot.

I got up at 5:00 the next morning for my quiet time. In the middle of my devotions, I heard something outside. As I looked out my window, I saw that the woman had set up a cage in a nearby tree and was down on her knees praying. I wondered if I had somehow led this woman into total delusion. Did she expect a wild parrot to just walk into the cage? Snickering, I returned to my quiet time. Later that morning I led a big prayer meeting, all filled with faith.

The following morning I got up for my quiet time again. This time I was in deep prayer for the World Prayer Center—the very thing for which I needed faith. Again, I heard something outside. I opened my window and looked to see this woman shutting the door of the cage. Inexplicably, a large, beautiful parrot had flown into the yard and walked into the waiting cage all on its own!

I looked up at the Lord and said, "Lord, I am in bad trouble for my lack of faith." And it just felt like He agreed with me.

NO MATTER WHERE YOU ARE IN LIFE, GOD HAS A PLAN TO INCREASE YOUR MEASURE OF FAITH!

That day the Lord began to speak into my heart and say, "Your borders are too narrow. But I can cross your borders, I can bring the supply that's needed. If you will have faith as a child, I will release that which you need in this hour." Today that parrot sits in my house. I can't look at it without being reminded of God's supply in the face of childlike faith. I encourage you that no matter where you are in life, God has a plan to increase your measure of faith!

SOME AREAS OF RESTORATION

In the last chapter, we established that God is longing to restore abundant *zoe* life to us—not just to a former state, but to a greater measure than we have ever known. The following are 10 specific areas that, as God works His restoration, will give us that vital, blessed, rich life worth living (many of these points will be covered in greater detail in later chapters).

1. OUR FREEDOM

"It is for freedom that Christ has set us free. Stand firm, then, and do not let yourselves be burdened again by a yoke of slavery" (Gal. 5:1, *NIV*). God longs for His people to be free from whatever chains have held them in bondage. In both the Old and New Testaments, God has proven this pattern to be so. The people of Israel, for example, cried out in agony when they were enslaved in Egypt. God heard their

groanings and remembered the promises He had given to their forefathers. The rest of the book of Exodus shows the extraordinary lengths to which God will go to set His people free and to keep His promises.

Later, we see how the prophet Jeremiah was freed from captivity and given several options. *"And now look, I free you this day from the chains that were on your hand. If it seems good to you to come with me to Babylon, come, and I will look after you. But if it seems wrong for you to come with me to Babylon, remain here. See, all the land is before you; wherever it seems good and convenient for you to go, go there"* (Jer. 40:4). The word "free" in this passage is the Hebrew word *pathach,* meaning to open wide, loosen, set free, release, untie, unshackle or liberate. Through that freedom, that *"pathach-*ing," Jeremiah was not only freed from the captivity he had been in, but he was then also able to make some choices and begin a whole new process in his life; shackles had been released and a new door had opened wide.

Of course the most beautiful example of freedom that directly affects each of us today was prophesied by Isaiah of the Lord Jesus, *"The Spirit of the Lord God is upon Me, because the Lord has anointed Me to preach good tidings to the poor; He has sent Me to heal the brokenhearted, to proclaim liberty to the captives, and the opening of the prison to those who are bound"* (Isa. 61:1).

Jesus releases and liberates us from the dominion of sin and restores us to a right relationship with the Father. When that happens, the hindrances of restoration are broken. Sin resists freedom, but Christ delivers us into a freedom that reverses our death sentence and starts life in motion!

We must, however, recognize that we are indeed free. I recently heard the story of a dog who had been tied to a post for some years. The dog would stretch to the end of its rope and walk in circles around the post. As the years passed, the dog trod out an entrenched circular groove in the earth. Though he could see much farther, his world could only reach as far as his restraints would let him.

One day, the dog's master decided to free him from the post. The man untied the rope and watched, expecting to see the dog race off into the surrounding area and explore that which he had only been allowed to view from his restrained position. Strangely, the dog did not run or play or explore. Though his master tried to entice him away, the dog merely began to walk in the entrenched circle he had created throughout such a long period of time.

We, like the dog, are often unaware that our restraints have been removed. Even when the Lord would try to move us out into our new freedom, we may have a tendency to remain in the safety of the entrenchments we have created for ourselves.

2. OUR PLACE OR POSITION

"'They shall be carried to Babylon, and there they shall be until the day that I visit them,' says the Lord. 'Then I will bring them up and restore them to this place'" (Jer. 27:22). This Scripture from Jeremiah refers to the captivity of the children of Israel in Babylon. God had made a covenant to bring them out of that captivity. So when the time came for their captivity to end, God determined to put them back on their road to success and establish them in a new place.

God will do the same for us. He earnestly desires to establish us in a physical place as a part of our inheritance.

3. OUR HEALTH

"'For I will restore health to you and heal you of your wounds,' says the Lord, 'Because they called you an outcast saying: "This is Zion; no one seeks her"'" (Jer. 30:17). As we discussed earlier in this chapter, through sin we have become fragmented and scattered in a way that can result in physical illness, even to the point of decreasing our life spans. But God is the Mighty Physician who will restore our health.

4. OUR JOY

"Restore to me the joy of Your salvation, and uphold me by Your generous Spirit" (Ps. 51:12). Our enemy longs to rob us of our joy and get us

out of the salvation process we discussed earlier in this chapter. That does not mean that he can steal our salvation by robbing our joy, but he can steer us away from the forgiveness, healing, prosperity and restoration that are by-products of our salvation. His strategy many times is the same one he used on King David: he causes us to sin. Nothing will rob us of the joy of the Lord as effectively as sin in our lives.

But these are days in which God is longing to restore joy to His people through deeper levels of repentance. In repairing the breaches that sin has caused, God is able to restore joy. Proverbs 17:22 says, *"A merry heart does good, like medicine."* Joy works like a medicine and brings healing to our bones. That is why Scripture says that the joy of the Lord is our strength (see Neh. 8:10); it brings with it the power to heal and maintain the health God has for us.

Even though David sinned and lost his joy, we see from Psalm 51 that he was able to ask the Lord to restore that joy to him. Through the blood of Christ, we are positioned with even greater favor than King David had to ask the Lord to forgive our transgressions and restore the joy of our salvation.

5. OUR INHERITANCE

"And may he be to you a restorer of life and a nourisher of your old age; for your daughter-in-law, who loves you, who is better to you than seven sons, has borne him" (Ruth 4:15). God is a restorer of life. A central issue to inheritance is a choice between life and death. As we choose to move forward in the *zoe* life God has for us, God will restore our inheritance.

In the story of Ruth, God restored inheritance to Naomi by establishing her place and sending her a kinsman redeemer. Naomi understood the plan of restoration in her life and moved toward it until all her inheritance was restored to her.

"Return to the stronghold, you prisoners of hope. Even today I declare that I will restore double to you" (Zech. 9:12). In this passage we see

how restoration and hope are linked. God is a God who returns His people into the fullness of hope. In this process God not only restores inheritance, but He also brings us into a greater portion than we had before!

6. OUR COVENANT RELATIONSHIP

Nehemiah 8 is a perfect example of a people who had lost their inheritance. God's people were a mess! Their walls, their city, even their lives had fallen into rubble. In their desperation, Ezra read the Word of the Lord to them. As they heard God's Word, the people realized the scope of their loss and began to weep. But that was not a time for weeping. God had instead ordained that the people have a Feast of Tabernacles and rejoice for one week.

When they obeyed God and feasted, they found their joy returning to them. The result was that they began to come back into agreement with God's plan and rejoiced over the truth of what God wanted to restore to them. They came back into agreement with the covenant God had established with them long ago.

God has a covenant relationship with each of His children that carries great power for restoration and blessing. We must understand and come into agreement with that covenant in order to see restored that which has fallen into rubble in our lives.

7. OUR SOULS

"The Lord is my shepherd; I shall not want. He makes me to lie down in green pastures; He leads me beside the still waters. He restores my soul; He leads me in the paths of righteousness for His name's sake" (Ps. 23:1-3). This familiar and beautiful Scripture is a great reminder that God is the restorer of our souls.

Through trauma, trials, circumstances or sin, our souls can be left fragmented. This kind of fragmenting can affect our God-given personalities. The personality God has given each one of us is a reflection of some part of Himself. Some may reflect His love for people; some may reflect His sense of order; some may reflect His endless compassion; others may reflect His ability to lead onward. Each one is good. After all, God designed it. But as we are wounded by circumstances, or as we choose to sin, our personalities—the souls of who we are—become distorted and fragmented, and in some cases may not even resemble what God intended us to be. God, however, can restore our souls to wholeness—so much so that the personality of God can shine through our personalities.

8. OUR PORTIONS

"And the Lord restored Job's losses when he prayed for his friends. Indeed the Lord gave Job twice as much as he had before" (Job 42:10). I love the story of Job. Even in his pain and loss, Job stayed focused in his understanding of God's character and nature. If the enemy had been allowed to kill him, we have sufficient evidence from Job's attitude to believe that he would still have loved and honored God. What a testimony.

It was as Job began to pray for his friends, who argued that his afflictions were a judgment, that God began to restore double to Job. Even when our portion is tested and seems to be lost, we must not assume that God has either forgotten or forsaken us. We must stay focused on who God is. We must also be assured that somewhere in our loss, God has a plan of multiplication.

9. THE LOST OR WANDERING SHEEP

"Brethren, if a man is overtaken in any trespass, you who are spiritual restore such a one in a spirit of gentleness, considering yourself lest you also be tempted" (Gal. 6:1). As we begin to understand and implement these principles of restoration, we are going to see God bring the prodigals back into the house of the Lord—specifically those who have been wounded by God's people.

In fact, I believe God is on the verge of bringing an entire prodigal generation to us. It is important that we understand God's desire for restoration for this generation. We must not respond as the Church responded in the '60s and '70s when God attempted to bring a generation in, only to be rejected by His people. We must empty ourselves of all hypocrisy, judgment and self-righteousness so He can begin to bring the lost sheep back. As we do, we will see many prodigals come to a place of restoration and carry His destiny into the next generation.

10. THE FATHER'S HEART

"And he will turn the hearts of the fathers to the children, and the hearts of the children to their fathers" (Mal. 4:6). The "father's heart" that the Lord is restoring is truly one of the most beautiful prophetic pictures of who God is. And a great resurgence of understanding for the role of "fathering" is occurring in the Body of Christ.

In the book *You Have Not Many Fathers*, Dr. Mark Hanby describes the father's heart this way:

> Here is the heart of a true father: His son should do better, know more, go farther. Often our personal desires and possessive love would cause them to stay where we are or have them fulfill our own dreams. Selfishly we would make them servant to our personal agendas. Yet every true dad knows that the day will come when his own dreams will drive away.[4]

A modern-day example of just such a man can be found in Dr. C. Peter Wagner, who has given leadership to the prayer movement of the '90s and is now emerging as a leading figure in this New Apostolic Reformation. In addition to being the natural father of Rebecca Wagner Sytsema, coauthor of this book, I have known and been mentored by him for many years. He has always displayed exactly the attitude alluded to by Mark Hanby.

On one occasion I recall reading evaluations from a conference Peter had just completed in which both he and Cindy Jacobs, to whom he is a spiritual father, had been plenary speakers. The evaluations rated him as a 10 and Cindy as a 10 plus. Peter could not have been prouder of Cindy. When I asked him about the scores, he replied that if those whom he has mentored did not score higher and achieve more in the kingdom of God than he, he would consider himself a failure as a father in the Kingdom. Peter doesn't care if Cindy ever recognizes him publicly. If she continues moving forward and accomplishing God's destiny for her, then he has been a successful father whose heart has been turned toward the children.

Notes

1. E. Anthony Allen, *Transforming Health*, Eric Ram, ed. (Monrovia, Calif.: Marc and World Vision International), p. 7.
2. Taken from Appendix 1, Elmer Towns, *The Names of the Holy Spirit*, (Ventura, Calif.: Regal Books, 1994), pp. 195-198.
3. Jack Hayford, *I'll Hold You in Heaven* (Ventura, Calif.: Regal Books, 1990), p. 90.
4. Mark Hanby, *You Have Not Many Fathers* (Shippensburg, Pa.: Destiny Image, 1996), p. 53.

T H R E E

FROM GRIEF TO GLORY

*Hope deferred makes the heart sick, but when the
desire comes, it is a tree of life.*

—PROVERBS 13:12

These are exciting times in which to be a Christian! In the decade of
the '90s, we have seen one of the greatest worldwide moves of God
in the history of Christianity. Many missiologists and Christian
leaders agree that the spark for the current renewal and revival
being experienced in various parts of the world has come from
Argentina.

In his book *Warfare Prayer* (Regal Books), Dr. C. Peter Wagner
describes how, through strategic-level spiritual warfare, the Lord
brought Argentina from a place of desolation to tremendous
revival. A major reason the revival fires in Argentina have
spread throughout the world is because of an annual conference
held in Argentina which is sponsored by Harvest Evangelism and

Ed Silvoso. The Harvest Institute gathers leaders from around the world, brings them to Argentina and exposes them to the tremendous move of God in that nation. Often these leaders have been so touched by the Holy Spirit while in Argentina that they have carried back a revival anointing to their own churches and regions.

In 1992, along with Bobbye Byerly, I was privileged to colead the intercession team for Harvest Institute. We had a small but powerfully unified team, including Esther Ilnisky, Keren Stoll and Rebecca Sytsema. As the five of us sought the Lord with great intensity, the Lord met us with an amazing breakthrough. During times of ministry, we saw the participants (most of whom were Evangelicals without the slightest charismatic bent) being deeply moved by the Holy Spirit—laughing, weeping and rolling on the floor. Few of us had ever seen such manifestations of the Holy Spirit. That is when I inquired of the Lord about what He was doing. At that moment as I stood and watched the outpouring of God's grace, He spoke deep in my spirit saying, "I am bringing My people from grief to glory!"

That phrase has stuck in my mind ever since. What does it mean to go from grief to glory? As I have studied and learned more, I have concluded that, first, this is the will of God for each of us and, second, there is a definite process involved. Let us examine closely the process we must go through—from the loss and grief that often comes in a wilderness season, through the transition and into the time of restoration. We'll begin by looking at the wilderness.

UNDERSTANDING THE WILDERNESS SEASONS

The wilderness...a place that many of us fear and would gladly avoid if given the opportunity. The wilderness evokes thoughts of a dry, thirsty place hosting thorny, spiked growth upon an endless blanket of infertile, parched land. The stillness of the atmosphere is isolating and broken only by vengeful, howling winds that carry irritating granules of sand to imperil vision and blister the skin. What little life there is in these impoverished places has to fight hard for existence, seeking out the few available drops of water that will bring another day's survival. Hardly an inviting picture. Yet, the wilderness is unavoidable; it's a principle of God. He created us to move through spiritual seasons just as He created the earth to move through physical seasons. And some of those seasons are spent in a wilderness.

HOW WE GET THERE

Wilderness seasons occur in one of three ways.

First, we enter through obedience to the God's leading. After His baptism, the Lord Jesus Christ was led by the Spirit into the wilderness to be tempted. Jesus' obedience in the wilderness both defeated Satan's plans to disqualify Him and thrust Him into His ministry (see Matt. 4). It is in the wilderness that we willingly follow the Lord into suffering in order to defeat the enemy and gain what we need to move into God's destiny for us.

Second, the wilderness season may be a result of sin. The Israelites were in just such a position. Even though they entered into the wilderness out of obedience, they sinned grievously against the Lord while there. God, therefore, promised to purge the sinful generation from them before they could enter into the Promised Land. Thus, they wandered for 40 years. Often God must purge sin issues from us before we can enter into the fullness of His promises.

The third way we enter into a wilderness season is by being thrust into it through circumstances beyond our control. Such was the case with Job. He experienced great loss, not as a result of sin or a choice he made, but as a result of being tested by God. Not every loss we suffer in our life is due to some cosmic wager, as it was with Job, but both God and Satan do watch our responses in wilderness seasons. Each one is looking for a chance: God is looking for a chance to restore and bless; Satan is looking for a chance to bring bondage that keeps us from moving forward.

How we respond in the wilderness determines our next season. If Moses had not disobeyed God in the wilderness, he would have been allowed to enter the Promised Land (see Num. 20:7-12). If Job had given in to grief and cursed God, he never would have come into the renewed blessing and restoration that God showered upon him (see Job 42:12); he would have died a bitter old man. If Christ had yielded to temptation, not only would He have missed His own destiny, but we too would have missed our only means of redemption!

We must participate with God's plan for our lives in order to step into the next season He has ordained for us. Yet we are often so overcome by grief in the wilderness season that we simply cannot move forward. How do we go from the painful reality of our own grief to the glory of God's restorative plan? To answer that question, we must first understand the basic principles of loss and restoration.

THE REALITY OF LOSS

As we've already discovered, experiencing loss is one way of entering into a wilderness season. Loss is a sad but unavoidable part of life. Whether it be through death, divorce, job loss, victimization, disabilities, property loss or a myriad of other tragedies and disappointments, everyone has experienced loss in one form or another. No one is immune. Therefore, it is important to understand what loss can do in our lives that will either move us toward a season of restoration, or keep us immobilized and lost in the wilderness.

LOSS PRODUCES GRIEF

All loss produces some kind of grief, which is the emotional expression of loss. Grieving is not an indication that a person is not spiritual, or somehow does not trust in God. In fact, many who have walked through intense grief have experienced a level of God's grace that they might never have known otherwise. God would not extend such grace to His children if He frowned on allowing us to grieve after a loss.

Experts in the field of human behavior tell us that there are, in fact, stages to the "normal" grieving process. These stages can include emotions such as shock, denial, bargaining, depression, anger, guilt, confusion, and finally hope and acceptance. Someone experiencing grief may go through all or only some of these emotions. Everyone is unique in dealing with pain.

The grieving process affects everyone differently, and two people may come out of the same situation with opposing frames of mind. Let's consider two widows, for example. The experience of widowhood may lead one woman to a deeper understanding of the Lord's husbandry as described in Isaiah 54:5, which says, *"For your Maker is your husband, the Lord of hosts is His name; and your Redeemer is the Holy One of Israel; He is called the God of the whole earth."* This woman, because of her widowhood, will reap a deeper relationship and reliance upon the Lord.

The other woman, however, may never quite get past the loneliness of her experience. She may live out her days without ever embracing full restoration from her painful loss.

There are two instances in which grief can keep us from moving toward restoration:

1. When the cycle of grief is not complete. Deep hurts require deep healing. And the healing process is usually longer and more strenuous than we ever expect. In fact, counselors will often refer to a person in the midst of recovering from loss as doing "grief work." This is a term used to describe a conscious decision to experience the emotions of grief as they come—no matter how uncomfortable they may be—and to see those emotions through to the end. The theory behind grief work is that as we allow ourselves to grieve through the ebb and flow of natural emotion, healing can begin to penetrate the pain. If we do not allow ourselves to heal and instead deny our emotions, the grief will fester and often manifest later in various harmful ways such as addictions, chronic depression, fits of anger or even physical illness.

We must also remember that we have an enemy who seizes our times of loss as opportunities to prey upon us. Unless we allow the Lord to take us through our seasons of grief and see them to the end, Satan can use our denial to create a stronghold of grief within our lives. It is often this kind of deeply embedded grief that keeps us from coming into restoration.

2. *When the cycle of grief goes on too long.* As necessary as grief may be, and as important as it is to see the process through, we can choose to grieve too long. Like the widow we just described, many people caught in the throws of pain can't see that there is a time to cast off mourning. Even the great prophet-priest Samuel fell into this comfortable grief trap as we see in 1 Samuel 16:1: *"Now the Lord said to Samuel, 'How long will you mourn for Saul?'"* God's appointed season of grieving for Samuel over Saul's removal from power had reached its limit. It was time for Samuel to either move on, or to miss the next move of God through David.

GOD'S GRACE COVERS OUR LACK OF NATURAL STRENGTH. BUT WHEN THE LORD IS READY TO MOVE US ON, THAT GRACE LIFTS. IF WE DO NOT MOVE WITH GOD, WE CAN BE LEFT IN A VULNERABLE AND WEAK PLACE, UNABLE TO CROSS OVER INTO OUR INHERITANCE.

Ecclesiastes 3:4 reminds us, *"There is...a time to weep, and a time to laugh; a time to mourn, and a time to dance."* Just as Satan can use denial to afflict us, he is equally adept at prolonging our seasons of grief far beyond what God intends. By keeping us feeling as though we are in a state of perpetual mourning, Satan knows that we cannot move into the abundant life God has for us beyond our loss. Grief robs us of strength—often the very strength we need to move into a season of life that is far greater than we had before the loss. During an appropriate season of grief, God's grace covers our lack of natural strength. But when the Lord is ready to move us on, that grace lifts. If we do not move with God, we can be left in a vulnerable and weak place, unable to cross over into our inheritance.

Joshua was a great leader in Israel. He was the one who actually led the children of Israel across the Jordan into Canaan and spearheaded the military campaigns that allowed the Israelites to possess the land God had promised. But what if Joshua had allowed his grief over the death of Moses to extend beyond the appointed season? Deuteronomy 34:8 says, *"And the children of Israel wept for Moses in the plains of Moab thirty days. So the days of weeping and mourning for Moses ended."* But what if the days of weeping and mourning had not ended? Very simply, Joshua would not have crossed over into God's inheritance for His people. His grief would have consumed the strength he needed for that vital hour in history. Instead, Joshua mourned appropriately, regained his strength, and moved on when the strategic time came.

A DEEPER HEALING

I believe that if we have ears to hear, God is faithful to show each of us when our seasons of mourning should come to an end—when it's time to cast off our robes of mourning and begin to live again. But when the time comes, does that mean we are totally healed? Not always. We may still experience pain from the losses in our lives. After all, these events do shape much of who we are. But feeling the pain and allowing the Lord to bring us to a deeper level of healing is not the same as living in mourning.

I had just such an experience in my own life. On February 6, 1988, my wife Pam gave birth to beautiful, full-term, identical-twin boys. We named our new sons, our precious gifts from God, Jesse David and Jacob Levi. But something in their tiny new bodies was very wrong. One of the babies had a serious heart problem; the other had a serious liver problem. Within one week, both of our

sons had died. The pain I felt over their deaths was almost overwhelming. I deeply mourned their loss. But God was faithful to see
me through that season and did, indeed, bring me out of mourning.

On July 22, 1997, Rebecca Sytsema lost her first baby (a daughter she and her husband named Anna Jean) in a stillbirth. Pam and
I have grown very close to both Becky and her husband, Jack, so
news of their daughter's death caused deep sadness in me for
them. But I found that through the death of their baby, grief over
the death of my own babies seemed to be rekindled. Because my
own pain was suddenly revisited, I knew the Lord was planning to
bring a deeper healing to my life, and He indeed has been doing
just that.

I have not been "in mourning" over the loss of my sons for the
nine years between these events. That season ended long ago. But
the process of healing from that trauma is still a reality in my life.
Even though the chronological season of grief may end, the process
of healing will go on until God's process of restoration is complete.

THE BENEFITS OF LOSS

*"And we know that all things work together for good to those who love God,
to those who are the called according to His purpose"* (Rom. 8:28).
God's purposes for us do not cease when we experience loss. In
fact, God may have a great purpose for us within our loss. This
familiar passage reminds us that our loss has not taken God by surprise. In fact, we may even find benefits that God has produced in
our lives through our painful experiences. Let's take a look at what
some of those benefits might be.

LOSS PRODUCES MATURITY

Even in the midst of life's greatest losses, God truly does have the
grace we need to see them through. As we choose to receive God's
grace in the midst of difficulty, we are able to reach a higher level of
perseverance, which grants us new hope for the future. Romans 5:3-5

says, *"And not only that, but we also glory in tribulations, knowing that tribulation produces perseverance; and perseverance, character; and character, hope. Now hope does not disappoint, because the love of God has been poured out in our hearts by the Holy Spirit who was given to us."*

God always has a way to see us through. But God's way is not simply a survival mode to gut the pain out. Not by any means. God's grace in times of grief helps us walk through the pain with hope for the future. In the times of deepest pain, grace is the lifeline we must grab with both hands. As we grab on to God's grace and hope, clarity begins to come in our situation, and great comfort can sweep over us. We reach a new level of maturity.

Gerald L. Sittser, associate professor of religion at Whitworth College in Spokane, Washington, is very familiar with this principle. In the fall of 1991, while driving home with his family, his minivan was hit head-on by a drunk driver. His mother, wife and young daughter were all killed in the accident. In his book *A Grace Disguised, How the Soul Grows Through Loss,* Sittser writes of his tragic experience and how God has helped him through it. He says:

> Above all, I have become aware of the power of God's grace and my need for it. My soul has grown because it has been awakened to the goodness and love of God....God is growing my soul, making it bigger, and filling it with Himself. My life is being transformed. Though I have endured pain, I believe that the outcome is going to be wonderful.
>
> The supreme challenge to anyone facing catastrophic loss involves facing the darkness of the loss on the one hand, and learning to live with renewed vitality and gratitude on the other. This challenge is met when we learn to take the loss into ourselves and to be enlarged by it, so that our capacity to live life well and to know God intimately increases....Loss can diminish us, but it can also expand us. It depends, once again, on the choices we make and the grace we receive. Loss can function as a catalyst to transform

us. It can lead us to God, the only One who has the desire and power to give us life.[1]

By reaching out toward God's wonderful grace, our loss can actually become a bittersweet blessing that leads us to knowing God on a deeper and more intimate level.

Though we mourn the loss, we gain a new maturity in life, and a deeper understanding of God's awesome grace and hope.

LOSS PRODUCES JOY

The Bible is full of references about mourning turned to joy. A few examples are:

> *For His anger is but for a moment, His favor is for life; weeping may endure for a night, but joy comes in the morning....You have turned for me my mourning into dancing; You have put off my sackcloth and clothed me with gladness* (Ps. 30:5,11).

> *As the days on which the Jews had rest from their enemies, as the month which was turned from sorrow to joy for them, and from mourning to a holiday; that they should make them days of feasting and joy, of sending presents to one another and gifts to the poor* (Esther 9:22).

> *For I will turn their mourning to joy, will comfort them, and make them rejoice rather than sorrow* (Jer. 31:13).

> *To console those who mourn in Zion, to give them beauty for ashes, the oil of joy for mourning, the garment of praise for the spirit of heaviness* (Isa. 61:3).

John 16:16-23 is a beautiful passage in which Jesus prophesies His own death and resurrection. Verses 20-22 speak directly of the sorrow and joy that the disciples were about to experience:

Most assuredly, I say to you that you will weep and lament, but the world will rejoice; and you will be sorrowful, but your sorrow will be turned into joy. A woman, when she is in labor, has sorrow because her hour has come; but as soon as she has given birth to the child, she no longer remembers the anguish, for joy that a human being has been born into the world. Therefore you now have sorrow; but I will see you again and your heart will rejoice, and your joy no one will take from you.

Sorrow and joy are firmly linked. Perhaps it is because the deeper we experience sorrow, the more capacity we have for joy. I suppose it is similar to hunger. The hungrier we are, the more satisfying a good meal is to us. God knows this. Although we may only see the sorrow and tears of the night, He has planned a bright and beautiful morning full of joy. Pam and I are so aware of this principle that we chose to put John 16:22 (previously quoted) on the headstone of our twin sons, knowing that one day our sorrow would turn to joy that no one could take from us.

One reason God may have for bringing joy after a season of sorrow is to bring a new wind of strength to our spirits. A few pages back, we looked at how grieving robs strength. There is a weakness that comes from such an emotional and spiritual load. But God knows that joy brings a new vitality and strength, *"for the joy of the Lord is your strength"* (Neh. 8:10). Joy produces the kind of strength we need to move into our next season.

Like the disciples at the crucifixion of Jesus, we may go through intense and even confusing losses. But, like the disciples at His resurrection, great joy awaits us that no one will be able to take away.

LOSS PRODUCES CHANGE

Once we've experienced loss, life is not the same. We are not the same. Depending on the loss, we may not be able to do things the way we could before. Our view of life changes. Our view of God changes. We are moved into a new season of having to deal with all the ways our loss affects us and those around us. Once again, Gerald Sittser offers insight:

> The experience of loss does not have to leave us with the memory of a painful event that stands alone, like a towering monument that dominates the landscape of our lives. Loss can also leave us with the memory of a wonderful story. It can function as a catalyst that pushes us in a new direction, like a closed road that forces us to turn around and find another way to our destination. Who knows what we will discover and see along the way?[2]

The search for another way to our destination can produce a wilderness season in our lives. It may feel as though we are wandering aimlessly, like the children of Israel who could not go back to Egypt, yet did not know where they were headed. But be assured that just as God was leading the children of Israel through the wilderness to their restoration, God is doing the same for us.

GOD'S RESPONSE TO LOSS IS ALWAYS RESTORATION IN SOME FORM.

LOSS PRODUCES RESURRECTION

Jesus rose in order to bring life into victory over death, which is God's ultimate restoration. With that picture in mind, we can be assured that when we experience loss, especially of something that was a part of our inheritance, God invariably has a plan for restoring it to us. When death comes, for example, God always longs to start a resurrection process. David W. Wiersby, in his book *Gone But Not Lost*, which was written to those grieving the death of a child, writes, "God's response to death is always life. That doesn't mean he gives another child when one dies. It means that out of the sorrow and ruin of your 'other' life, God gives you a new life."[3] The same is true for any loss. God's response to loss is always restoration in some form.

Now let's take a look at the next step in moving out of the wilderness into a season of restoration.

THE NARROW PLACE OF TRANSITION

"Who is this coming out of the wilderness like pillars of smoke, perfumed with myrrh and frankincense, with all the merchant's fragrant powders?" (Song of Sol. 3:6).

God has a time for us to rise up out of the wilderness. But like the wilderness season, the season of transition is another place many of us would love to avoid. In fact, because of this season many people never move into all that God has for them. Yet it is transition that moves us from the wilderness into our restoration. But transition is usually the most difficult of all seasons. Because transition means crossing over to a new place or passing from one condition to another, we often have to travel through a "narrow place" as we venture through the process.

The narrow place is where the paths we are used to walking suddenly becomes more confined and precarious—much like crossing over a deep ravine on a swinging bridge. During these confining times, we commonly find ourselves under the Lord's scrutiny. But God always has a purpose. He tests us in the difficult places so He can trust us with new stewardship.

In Luke 18 we find the story of the rich, young ruler who asked the Lord what he should do to inherit eternal life. The young ruler was a religious young man who was genuinely seeking the right path. Yet when Jesus told him to take the narrow path of selling all he had in order to follow Him, the young man could not do it and left Jesus without receiving eternal life. Jesus then declared that it would be easier for a camel to go through the eye of a needle than for those who have riches to enter into the kingdom of God.

The "eye of a needle" that Jesus was referring to was a particularly narrow opening in the wall near one of the main gates of Jerusalem. A camel could only get through the opening by being stripped of all it carried, dropping to its knees and remaining on its knees to literally crawl through the opening. The young man refused to be stripped of all he had in order to go through the narrow place that led to eternal life. Yet if we are to get through the narrow place successfully, we must often unload what we are carrying, including weights of the past and old mind-sets.

During the narrow place of transition, the Lord often redefines and adjusts whatever rules are necessary for us to get to our new place. A good example of this is when Moses died and the mantle of authority was passed on to Joshua. Up to that point in the journey, the Israelites had learned to follow a pillar of cloud in the day and a pillar of fire by night. But now the Lord commanded them to follow the ark, a small box. What a shift! Their vision literally had to change from seeing the large moving pillars to focusing on a small box carried far ahead of them on the shoulders of priests. They had to become more focused in their place of transition. Often, in our own place of transition, we too must become much more focused on the Lord in order to make it through to the place of restoration that God has for us.

Transition is, therefore, a time when we must carefully hear what the Lord is saying to us. God has a strategy for you to make it through. He may be shifting you from following a large pillar that fills the horizon to focusing on a small, distant ark. The only way to clearly know His strategy for your particular situation is to spend time with Him.

A TIME OF BIRTH

Another picture of the narrow place of transition is that of a woman giving birth. My wife Pam and I have five beautiful children.

Although I have not had to physically give birth to them, I have coached my wife many times. She, and most women who give birth, will tell you that "transition" is the most difficult time in the birthing process. It is the most intense, painful part. During transition, many women feel as if they can't go on. Only the hope of the child to come gives them the endurance to press through and give birth. One textbook on pregnancy describes transition this way:

> Not surprisingly, at this point you may feel exhausted. Emotionally, you may feel vulnerable and overwhelmed; you're reaching the end of your rope. In addition to frustration, you may feel discouraged, irritable, disoriented, (and) restless.[4]

The transition seasons in life can bear great resemblance to the birthing process. Many of us "lose it" during this time. Satan loves to hit God's people with great force when we are in a season of transition because that's the time when we feel weakened and vulnerable. But if we come to a greater understanding of the process of transition, we can make it through transition with victory. We can bring to birth that with which God longs to bless us.

UNDERSTANDING THE TRANSITION PROCESS

Unquestionably, transition is a hard place. But if we can understand three important facts about this season, we can make it through with greater confidence.

1. There is an ending. God does not leave us in that narrow, pressed place longer than is necessary. He does have a time for it to end. Psalm 66:10-12 describes the process, *"For You, O God, have tested us; You have refined us as silver is refined. You brought us into the net; You laid affliction on our backs. You have caused men to ride over our heads; we went through fire and through water; **but You brought us out to rich fulfillment**"* (emphasis added).

Another passage of Scripture tells of the end of Israel's captivity in Babylon. *"For thus says the Lord: After seventy years are completed at Babylon, I will visit you and perform My good word toward you, and cause you to return to this place. For I know the thoughts that I think toward you, says the Lord, thoughts of peace and not of evil, to give you a future and a hope"* (Jer. 29:10,11).

God longs to restore. His desire is to bring us out into rich fulfillment and to complete His good word toward us. He wants to bring us into new stewardship and a deeper walk with Him. In order for that to happen, the trying, painful seasons must come to an end. Transition is temporary. God has bountiful seasons ahead for those who will seek Him in the narrow place. In times of transition remember the words of Paul who writes, *"forgetting those things which are behind and reaching forward to those things which are ahead, I press toward the goal for the prize of the upward call of God in Christ Jesus"* (Phil. 3:13,14). A new season is just ahead!

2. Confusion in transition is normal. Romans 8:7 says that our carnal mind is in enmity against God. Therefore, all the old carnal mind-sets that we need to put away in order to make it through the narrow place begin to resist the season in which God has placed us. Because our minds cannot comprehend what the new place will look like, and because the rules may be changing—just as they did for the children of Israel who had to follow the ark instead of the pillars—our minds come into opposition against the narrow place. Things look and feel so different that we can easily begin to wonder if God is really in all that we are experiencing. We begin to think: *The pillars of cloud and fire were working just fine so why would God go and change it now?* Is it His intention to confuse us and cause us to wonder? No. But it is our nature to resist change and look to what has worked in the past. If that old method or mind-set is no longer appropriate for where God is taking us, but we refuse to give it up, confusion can easily grip our minds.

Secular expert in the field of transitions William Bridges refers to this phase as the "neutral zone." He describes the feelings this way: "For many people the experience of the neutral zone is essentially one of emptiness in which the old reality looks transparent and nothing feels solid any more."[5] The feelings of confusion and even apprehension are very normal emotions. We can't go back to the comfort of where we were, and we don't know what lies ahead.

Children of God, however, have a distinct advantage during this phase of transition. Even though our emotions may be stirred and our minds full of anxious questions or disquieting scenarios, we can remain calm in the knowledge that God knows exactly where He wants to lead us. New challenges may confront us but so will riches that we have not experienced before. Therefore, we must trust that God knows what can and cannot follow us into the new season. We need to ask the Lord to show us what we should leave behind. For if we, like the young ruler who encountered Jesus, will not unload what we do not need in order to cross over into the new, we will not make a successful transition. We will have to turn back into the wilderness for another season.

Confusion in the process is normal. God does not condemn us for it. But we must work to get past our confusion by spending time inquiring of the Lord. As Joshua took his place of leadership, the Lord urged Joshua not to fear, but to instead meditate day and night upon Him and His covenant promises which He had spoken throughout the ages. As Joshua was faithful to obey, God showed him the new method for the new season. Only through Joshua's time with the Lord could God reveal His new method for leading the children of Israel, not by pillars, but by an ark.

God is the same today. If we will spend time with Him, remembering the promises He has made to us and inquiring about those things that cause us confusion, He will be faithful to bring us clarity. Our new clarity will not only lead us out of transition, but will also give us what we need for our new place. This is how we put on the mind of Christ—how our minds are renewed.

3. There is a new beginning. Transition does not last forever. There comes a time when the narrow place begins to enlarge once more. God starts bringing times of refreshing and restoration, without which we could not accomplish our future calls. When we can sense a new beginning on the horizon, we know God is preparing a season of restoration for us. We must remember, however, that moving into the new season is not automatic. Moving forward into the restoration God has depends on how we respond in the time of transition. William Bridges says, "Genuine beginnings begin within us, even when they are brought to our attention by external opportunities. It is out of the formlessness of the neutral zone that new form emerges and out of the barrenness of the fallow time that new life springs."[6]

THE SEASON OF RESTORATION

It may come dramatically, or it may be imperceptible at first—almost unimpressive. But sure enough, one day we find that the shifting has occurred and that we have moved solidly into the new season.

Finally! After coming through the wilderness and navigating through transition, we have moved on. Coming into this new season, however, does not mean that we are exempt from difficulties or issues to resolve. The refining process we go through as Christians never ends, but the dry, hard seasons do. The grief subsides and clarity comes. Then we can take a deep breath and look at the future with more peace and confidence.

FROM GRIEF TO GLORY

Most of us are fairly secure with our salvation, and yet we never come into the abundance that God has for us. That is simply because we are not whole. Our lives are like a sieve allowing God's abundance to leak out, even when He attempts to pour it in. We are the old wineskins that cannot contain the rich new wine. But as we submit to the process described in this chapter, a wholeness develops within us. From that wholeness comes the rich abundance that Jesus promised to bring us through *zoe* life.

God never intended for us to be fragmented, defeated people. His desire is to restore and to bless with great abundance. Scripture states that His intent is for us to move from glory to glory. But first God moves us from the grief we often find ourselves in to the glory He has for us. The prophet in Haggai 2 describes the transition as a great shaking that must occur in our lives. God promises, however, that the fruit of that shaking will be that the glory of the latter house will be greater than the former!

Notes

1. Gerald L. Sittser, *A Grace Disguised* (Grand Rapids, Mich.: Zondervan Publishing, 1996), pp. 180, 181.
2. Ibid., p. 130.
3. David W. Wiersby, *Gone But Not Lost* (Grand Rapids, Mich.: Baker Book House, 1992), p. 111.
4. Arlene Eisenberg, Heidi E. Murkoff, Sandee E. Hathaway, *What to Expect When You're Expecting* (New York, N.Y.: Workman Publishing, 1991), p. 297.
5. William Bridges, *Transitions, Making Sense of Life's Changes* (Reading, Ma.: Addison-Wesley Publishing Company, 1980), p. 117.
6. Ibid., p. 145.

FROM GLORY TO GLORY

But we all, with unveiled face, beholding as in a
mirror the glory of the Lord, are being transformed
into the same image from glory to glory, just
as by the Spirit of the Lord.

—*2 CORINTHIANS 3:18*

THE GLORY OF GOD

As children of God, part of our inheritance is experiencing the glory of God and being transformed into new levels of His glory. Each level of glory carries with it a particular blessing and thrill for us as Christians. In an effort to understand the glory of God, let's look at both the aspect of experiencing and the aspect of being transformed into His glory.

EXPERIENCING THE GLORY OF GOD

To experience the glory of God is to experience His manifest presence. It is to go beyond an abstract understanding of His omnipresence to knowing that God Himself is there with you, tangibly in your midst. In his book, *Glory on Your House*, Jack Hayford describes experiencing the glory of God this way:

> This does not mean you have to have a vision of something visible, as I did. God may be noticeably present in glory and power without any such manifestation. The Hebrew word translated "glory" helps us grasp this, in that it is also the word for "weight." When the Bible speaks of "the glory," it is not speaking so much of something aglow as of something with substantial force to it. Glory isn't something flimsy, ethereal, intangible. Rather, when the glory of God is in a place, something forceful, weighty, mighty is present in the spiritual realm. People can recognize it. They will want to be there. Mankind longs intuitively for the fulfillment and restoration, the focus and fruitfulness, that attend the soul reintroduced to lost glory.[1]

The "weight" that Hayford refers to here is the Hebrew word *kabod*, which implies not only heaviness, but a great quantity of things. The *New Unger's Bible Dictionary* (Moody Press) defines glory as the manifestation of God's attributes and perfections, or a visible splendor that represents His attributes or perfections. It can be said, then, that the glory of God is the full weight and quantity of His attributes and perfections. The glory of God is essentially what He is and does.

One way to experience God's glory is to experience a tangible manifestation of one or more of His attributes, such as an overwhelming sense of His utter holiness when all we can do is bow and worship Him in awe. Or we may experience a great sweep of His joy that brings deep refreshing to our spirits. Each of us who have been born again have experienced the glory of His saving grace, perhaps the most precious gift of all. We may catch a fresh glimpse of His mighty power, causing new faith to arise within us. Every one of these experiences, and so many others we could describe, is a manifestation of God's glory.

These kinds of experiences may be quiet occurrences in our personal devotional times, or in the middle of a prayer meeting or church service. Sometimes, however, a manifestation of His glory may be a dramatic, supernatural manifestation of God, much as it was for me when I was 18 years old. His voice was so loud and clear that it seemed audible to me. I can quote the very words. In my case, that visitation changed the course of my entire life.

In *Glory on Your House,* Jack Hayford describes a vision he had of the glory of the Lord which appeared as a silvery mist with a glowing quality that filled the little sanctuary where he was standing alone. He likened it to the *shekinah*—the radiant visible manifestation of God's glory described in the Bible. He then heard the voice of God say, "I have given My glory to dwell in this place." At that time the small church Hayford pastored barely averaged 100. The day after this visitation 170 came to the little church.[2]

Since that day years ago, although not manifested in a silvery mist, the glory of the Lord has continued to shine on The Church On The Way and Jack Hayford. More than 10,000 worshipers attend this life-giving church on an average Sunday. Dozens if not scores of new believers come to know the Lord there each month. Hayford's worldwide recognition as a modern-day father in the faith continues to gain in strength and credibility. That dramatic manifestation of God's glory changed not only the course of his small church, but also the course of countless lives that have been so profoundly influenced by one man's ministry.

When God's manifest presence invades our daily lives, things change! We cannot remain the same. Either we will harden our hearts, as the Israelites did on many occasions, or we experience new *zoe* life. If we choose to allow God's presence to soften our hearts, then we may see the power of God released in greater measure. We may catch a glimpse of the very atmosphere of heaven. We experience God! He longs to pour out His glory upon His people so that we may know Him. This experience is not just for us personally, but for the harvest of souls the Lord would draw in through the magnetic influence His presence has on the lost.

BECOMING TRANSFORMED BY HIS GLORY

Becoming transformed by the glory of God may be a new thought to some. But, in fact, it is central to the Christian life. The reason is simple. The very character and ways of God were exhibited through Jesus as He walked the earth. Jesus was the incarnation of God's glory, weighted heavily with divine attributes.

Second Corinthians 4 says, *"They don't understand the message we preach about the glory of Christ, who is the exact likeness of God....For God, who said, 'Let there be light in the darkness,' has made us understand that this light is the brightness of the glory of God that is seen in the face of Jesus Christ"* (vv. 4,6, *NLT*).

Christ is our hope of glory (see Col. 1:27). Through Him we are being made into carriers of the glory of God. As believers in Christ, we are to be in a position of being transformed into the image of Christ—and that means mirroring the glory, or characteristics, of God. Second Corinthians 3:18 in the *New Living Translation* says, *"And all of us have had that veil removed so that we can be mirrors that brightly reflect the glory of the Lord. And as the Spirit of the Lord works within us, we become more and more like him and reflect his glory even more."*

This, of course, does not mean we will have the divine attributes that belong only to God (such as omniscience or omnipresence), but it does include such things as love, joy, peace, wisdom, mercy, justice, selflessness, patience, self-control, holiness and so forth. Therefore, as the Holy Spirit helps us move through the process of becoming more like Christ, we are moving from glory to glory!

WHY DO WE MOVE FROM GLORY TO GLORY?

The question comes up: Why is it necessary to move from glory to glory? Isn't one glory as good as the next? The answer is no.

The reason is because in every season of glory, we experience a new order that God brings to our lives as we mirror His image to a greater extent. But then we begin to add a new method—a settled plan or strategy of how we operate within that new order, which is our way of implementing what we have learned from God.

While in and of itself this is not a problem, we can eventually

---

AS THE HOLY SPIRIT MOVES US TOWARD BECOMING MORE CHRISTLIKE, THE METHODOLOGY OF AN OLD SEASON WILL NOT PROPEL US INTO THE FUTURE.

---

get so organized in God's last manifestation of glory that the enemy can use it to hold us back from God's next step. We must resist the temptation to become legalistic, or build binding doctrines around a truth that God revealed during a season of glory, because these tenets can prevent us from moving forward when the time comes for God to change the seasons in our lives. If we do not allow God to move us from glory to glory, we will get caught up in living in an old season. As the Holy Spirit moves us toward becoming more Christlike, the methodology of an old season will not propel us into the future. We need something new and fresh. We need a new glory.

PRAISE AND WORSHIP PRODUCE GLORY

All throughout God's Word, we see that God is enthroned in praise. We glorify Him through our worship. That is why praise and worship are essential to experiencing God's glory. Praise is that element of celebration that can transport us into the throne room of God. Once we are in the throne room at His feet, we need to worship and adore Him. As we worship Him in that intimate place, He begins to reveal His glory to us.

God is looking for true worshipers who will worship *"in spirit and truth"* (John 4:24). And as He finds those worshipers, they are able to experience the reality of heaven, which is God's glory.

GLORY AND INHERITANCE

So what does glory have to do with inheritance? It is at the very core. We are joint heirs with Christ. Glory, therefore, is part of our inheritance. Romans 8:17,18 says, *"And if children, then heirs—heirs of God and joint heirs with Christ, if indeed we suffer with Him, that we may also be glorified together. For I consider that the sufferings of this present time are not worthy to be compared with the glory which shall be revealed in us."*

So how does the Holy Spirit take us through this process of possessing our inheritance by moving from glory to glory? The following are some ways.

IT'S "DEW" TIME

"For the seed shall be prosperous, the vine shall give its fruit, the ground shall give her increase, and the heavens shall give their dew—I will cause the remnant of this people to possess all these" (Zech. 8:12).

Recently I had a dream in which I was walking in a thick, blue mist. I asked the Lord what the mist was. I sensed the Lord saying, "It is dew. You have entered a new season; it is 'dew' time." Knowing that the color blue signifies truth in the Word of God, I realized God was trying to release a revelation of truth for today. I then began to study "dew," and I believe the Lord revealed many correlations between the effects of dew on the earth and how He desires to move us to our next manifestation of His glory.

1. Dew renews the face of the earth. During the night when dew falls on the earth, vegetation is nourished and grows. Without dew, dryness and desolation can set in, greatly inhibiting the growth process. The same is true of renewal in the Lord. We are being renewed day by day, which suggests that an ongoing renovation, restoration and transformation is happening in our hearts and lives. Titus 3:5 says, *"According to His mercy He saved us, through the washing of regeneration and renewing of the Holy Spirit."* Just as dew regenerates and renews the earth, so the Holy Spirit regenerates and renews us.

The dew of renewal also brings a complete change of heart. The dew, though only a fine mist, is often enough to soften hard and otherwise barren ground. This is the same concept as the new wineskin, softened with oil. The Holy Spirit, God's restorative agent on this earth, can transform and renew through the quiet spiritual soaking of the dew of renewal. He needs only our cooperation, through obedient and submissive relationship with Him, to soak us afresh with the dew of renewal.

2. Heavenly dew provides strength to move forward. Dew is released when all is still. It does not gather when there is heat or wind. When the temperature falls, the air comes to a point of rest, then the dew can begin to cover the earth.

Rest occurs when we enter into the perfect will of God. If we will get still before the Lord, we will receive the revelation and strategy to move forward out of the hassles, anxieties and warfare that have sapped our strength in the past season.

The opposite of stillness is haste. Haste leads to poverty and lost inheritance because we misunderstand or are not willing to wait for God's strategy for our next step forward. *"But those who wait on the Lord shall renew their strength; they shall mount up with wings like eagles, they shall run and not be weary, they shall walk and not faint"* (Isa. 40:31). Isaiah 30:15 says, *"In quietness and confidence shall be your strength."* As we get quiet and rest before the Lord, we are in a much better position to hear and understand the strategy of our next step. In the process, His dew of refreshing can fall on our lives and bring new levels of strength that will move us forward.

3. The dew of the Holy Spirit imparts overcoming power. *"His heavens shall also drop dew....Your enemies shall submit to you, and you shall tread down their high places"* (Deut. 33:28, 29). By appropriating the power of God through the Holy Spirit (which in this passage is likened to dew), we have the authority to dethrone the enemy's plan to keep us from spiritual life and wholeness. High places in the Bible are often linked with places of sin and iniquity; places of idolatrous altars. We all have or have had high places in our lives filled with sin and iniquity, sometimes even passed down to us through the generations.

The dew of the Lord, used here as a picture of washing us clean, gives us the power to tread down the high places and defeat old enemies living there. This overcoming power allows God to break our conformity to the standards of this world, and renew our minds. He is able to replace old deceptions that have caused us to fail in the past with a new belief system that will bring us to success!

4. The refreshing dew of the Lord uncovers new supply and provision. *"'Therefore may God give you of the dew of heaven, of the fatness of the earth, and plenty of grain and wine.'...Then Isaac his father answered and said to him: 'Behold, your dwelling shall be of the fatness of the earth, and of the dew of heaven from above'"* (Gen. 27:28,39). When Isaac blessed Jacob, he equated the dew of heaven to the material prosperity that Jacob would receive.

Like the rain, dew was regarded in biblical times as God's gift, bringing good harvest and providing food. As the Israelites wandered in the wilderness, we find that God supplied their needs each night as the dew fell. *"Now the manna was like coriander seed, and its color like the color of bdellium. The people went about and gathered it, ground it on millstones or beat it in the mortar, cooked it in pans, and made cakes of it; and its taste was like the taste of pastry prepared with oil. And when the dew fell on the camp in the night, the manna fell on it"* (Num. 11:7-9). Dew, therefore, came to symbolize supply and provision, new every morning.

As we follow the Lord's leading, His dew will also rain down new supply and provision in our lives, just as it did for the children of Israel.

5. The favor of God is "like dew on the grass" (Prov. 19:12). Favor means pleasure, desire, delight, to be pleased with or favorable toward something. When God is pleased with us, His favor rests on us. Favor is very similar to grace and to glory. When we respond to the sovereign hand of God, He begins to drop down on us His favor. His favor can cause us to accomplish things on the earth and give us access to places that we did not previously have access to.

The opposite of favor is reproach, which means to find fault with, blame, criticize, disapprove of or discredit. As God's favor comes upon us, He removes condemnation, judgmentalism, failure, mistakes from the past—places where the enemy has brought reproaches into our lives. We exchange disapproval for favor.

God is raising up an obedient people who are responding to His heart. As we obey Him in faith (for without faith it is impossible to please God or allow His favor to come on us), we will begin to feel His favor dropping like dew from heaven.

6. Dew is not permanent. Dew falls during the night season when all is quiet and calm. As soon as the new morning breaks, however, the dew begins to evaporate. Our seasons, like the dew, are a process of moving from glory to glory. We cannot settle into all that the dew brings and expect it to last beyond the time God would allow.

The children of Israel received just enough manna for one day. The earth receives just enough dew to be refreshed for a short season. In the same way, we cannot allow ourselves to settle into our current state of glory. If we do, we will find that God is moving in a new way, or interrupting us with a circumstance, problem or even a vision that we can't control or engineer with our present understanding.

We need to move to our next place of glory. For that we must receive new revelation from God. If you are in a place of confusion, listen for God's voice to receive the necessary instructions that will bring new order to your life and circumstances. Don't fear changes! His glory falls like dew.

VISITATION

How do we receive revelation from God for our next step in order to move to our next glory? How do we listen for the voice of God? The answers often come from a visitation of the Holy Spirit. What I mean by a visitation from God is simply hearing from Him. By no means does your visitation need to be as dramatic as it was for me when I was 18. Like the apostle Paul, I needed to be arrested in my tracks in order for God to set me on the right course. Nor does it need to be like Jack Hayford's "silvery mist" vision. God does not visit all people in those ways. But visitation is a valid, legitimate part of Christian life. For us to fully possess our inheritance, we need to understand more about visitation and to be open to receiving His visits.

MY TIMES OF VISITATION

I have experienced many personal visitations from the Lord. And every visitation has resulted in a profound change in my path as well as in my understanding. In chapter 1 I told the story of God's hospital visit when I was 18 and how it dramatically changed my future direction.

Later, I will share two other times of visitation when the Lord revealed principles regarding sin and generational curses to both me and my wife Pam. Without an understanding of those principles I would never be able to fulfill the destiny God has for me or my family.

The following is one story of how I experienced both a divine and evil visitation that propelled me into a prayer life that has never been the same.

A SEASON OF FERVENT INTERCESSION

Some years ago I was living in Houston, Texas. At that time God had put our church into a new prayer focus initiated by an incoming pastor. This pastor asked the deacons (of which I was one) to begin praying together regularly with the prayer partner he had assigned to each of us. It did not take many times of prayer together before I realized that God was trying to do a whole new work in my partner's life; thus I began to intercede regularly for him on my own. I found myself praying that God's ultimate plan would unfold and transform him so he would accomplish all the purposes God had destined for him.

As I interceded for this deacon, the Lord began to reveal to me what His will was for this man's life. Each time I gained a clearer picture of God's direction for him, my intercession became more intense. As I prayed for him, a peculiar thing happened. God began to show me in detail what the destiny for my own life was to be!

My prayer life became electric. I would sometimes find myself praying several hours each night for many different things that I knew were on the heart of God. I prayed for the city of Houston. I prayed for my family and friends. I seemed to know God's will for their lives, so I would pray for it to become reality. I had the privilege of seeing God move, and the things I was praying for come to pass on many occasions. My spirit had become accessible to the purposes of God, and He was able to use me in strategic intercession.

AN EVIL VISITATION

During this glorious season, a strange thing happened. I received what I can only describe as a visitation from the enemy. It was in our bedroom at about 2 A.M. Something woke me from a sound sleep. As I looked around, I saw a dark, visible presence in the room. Though it had a tangible, physical form, I knew it was an evil-spirit being. The hideous creature spoke to me and said, "I command you to stop praying!"

I sat straight up in bed and with boldness said, "You have no right to be in here. I will not stop praying until I see God's purposes accomplished in whatever He wants me to pray for."

By this point my wife was awake, the dog was barking, and chaos seemed to pierce what had been a peaceful night only moments before. In that moment, I realized that this was nothing but a fear tactic the enemy was using to keep me from pressing in to the intercession God had called me to. Becoming angry, I pointed my finger at the evil presence and said, "I command you to leave this house. You have no right to try to instill fear in me or in my household!" With that, the creature was gone.

FOREVER CHANGED BY THE GLORY OF GOD

As soon as that evil presence left our room, a beautiful thing happened. Peace came flooding into our home, and though it was the middle of the night, our room lit up with a shining bright light. The light of God's glory had come down and manifested in our room! We were awestruck by the divine, glowing presence that had so quickly replaced the ugly evil that had just been expelled.

THE ENEMY WILL ATTEMPT TO SEND DISTRACTIONS, DIVERSIONS OR EVEN EVIL VISITATIONS TO KEEP US FROM EXPERIENCING THE GLORY OF GOD. HE KNOWS THAT ONCE GOD MANIFESTS HIS PRESENCE TO YOU, YOU BEGIN TO ADVANCE IN HIS STRENGTH AND IN HIS DESTINY FOR YOU.

The incident that night forever changed my prayer life. I knew then, beyond a shadow of a doubt, that prayer had real power and that Satan hated it. I also learned that God's reality from heaven will manifest as we submit ourselves to Him and resist the devil (see Jas. 4:7). When we resist the enemy, not only does he have to flee, but our resistance opens up a way for God to reveal Himself to us anew—whether through revelation, His manifest presence, the Scriptures or by some other means.

I also learned that the enemy will attempt to send distractions, diversions or even evil visitations to keep us from experiencing the glory of God. He knows that once God manifests His presence to you, you begin to advance in His strength and in His destiny for you. Satan's kingdom is threatened by you, and he will try to stop you. Even so, the scriptural principle of James 4:7 holds true, as I discovered one night in Houston.

FIVE OBSERVATIONS CONCERNING VISITATION

Over time, certain truths about visitation have been impressed upon me. Look with me at five particular observations that might help us better understand the topic:

1. There is a time of visitation. In the New Testament, two Greek words are used for time. One is *chronos*; the other is *kairos*. The word *chronos* refers to chronological time—days, weeks, months, years. *Kairos* refers to an appointed time or an opportune time. For instance, when a woman is pregnant, she spends nine months of *chronos* time in pregnancy, waiting for her child. But when she goes into labor, the *kairos* time for the birth of her child has come.

The Lord has set aside "appointed" or *kairos* times for visitation. When speaking prophetically to the city of Jerusalem, Jesus said, *"For days will come upon you when your enemies will build an embankment around you, surround you and close you in on every side, and level you, and your children within you, to the ground; and they will not leave in you one stone upon another,* **because you did not know the time of your visitation***"* (Luke 19:43,44, emphasis added).

In his book *Welcoming a Visitation of the Holy Spirit*, Wesley Campbell says:

God visited Jerusalem many times. His voice came through His prophets. His glory came in *kairos* events, such as the building of the temples. Finally, He came through His Son,

Jesus Christ, who boldly stated: "Anyone who has seen me has seen the Father" (John 14:9). However, after only three years of ministry, Jesus was forced to declare that enemies would raze the holy city of Jerusalem to the ground as judgment for not recognizing Him, even when He came in the flesh (see Luke 19:41-44). The prophesied judgment happened in A.D. 70 when Jerusalem was destroyed by the Roman invader, Titus.[3]

Jerusalem missed its time of visitation and, consequently, the people could not even recognize the Lord when He stood in their midst. Likewise, if we do not perceive our times of visitation, how will we recognize the Lord if He stands in our midst? We must realize that the Lord desires to bring visitation to us, and we must stand ready for our *kairos* times.

2. During times of visitation, miraculous blessings come. By far, the greatest visitation of God in history was the 33 years Jesus walked on earth. As Jesus moved among the people, tremendous blessings, on an unprecedented scale, fell on those with whom He came in contact. The blind received sight, the deaf heard, the lame walked, the dead were raised, sin was forgiven, bondages were broken, demoniacs were freed, and death, hell and the grave were soundly defeated.

As the Lord comes in contact with us today, why should we expect less? Miraculous blessings are a part of *kairos* times of visitation. We should cry out to God for visitations. Consider the story of blind Bartimaeus who, as Jesus was passing by, cried out for Him (see Mark 10:46-52). Others tried to quiet him, but Bartimaeus shouted even louder. Jesus, hearing him cry out, called to Bartimaeus and asked what he wanted Jesus to do for him. When Bartimaeus asked to receive his sight, Jesus said, *"Go your way; your faith has made you well"* (v. 52). Bartimaeus recognized the *kairos* time of Jesus' visitation. He also knew that if he did not cry out then, Jesus might not pass by again, and the chance to be healed would be lost.

Like blind Bartimaeus, we too must be ready for our visitations and willing to cry out to God for the miracles we need.

3. Faithfulness and consistency produce surprise visitations. In Luke 1:15—2:13, we read the story of the priest Zacharias who was righteous and blameless in the sight of the Lord. He was a good man who followed God's commandments and faithfully fulfilled the duties of his priesthood. But he and his wife Elizabeth had no children. Apparently Zacharias had petitioned the Lord concerning their barrenness. One day, while performing his normal priestly duties, an angel of the Lord visited him, told him that his petition had been heard and said that Elizabeth would bear a son whom they were to name John.

By no biblical indications were Zacharias or Elizabeth extraordinary people. But they were a man and woman of God who were found righteous in His sight. They were also faithful and consistent with the portion God had given them. It was in the consistent performance of Zacharias's duties that his *kairos* time of visitation came, and his prayer for a child was answered.

No one can know when a time of visitation is coming. But our faithfulness in serving in the portion God has given us and crying out to God for those barren places in our lives can be a catalyst to visitation—when we least expect to hear from Him.

4. Visitation secures our inheritance. *"Thou hast granted me life and favour, and thy visitation hath preserved my spirit"* (Job 10:12, *KJV*). The Hebrew word for "preserved" in this passage is *shamar*, meaning to guard, keep safe, protect, watch over or care for. The same word is used in Genesis 2:15 when Adam was called to tend and keep (*shamar*) the garden. *Shamar* is also used when God commanded His people to guard the covenant (see Gen. 17:9; Exod. 31:14; Deut. 28:9).

Here in Job we see that God has granted life and favor, and that His visitation has preserved (*shamared*) Job's spirit. Every time the will of God comes from heaven to earth and God's glory is present, our destiny, our inheritance, our very spirit is guarded, protected, watched over—*shamared* by the Spirit of God through that visitation. How? When visitation comes, God always releases some kind of strategic information that thrusts us forward in His purposes. As we respond to His visitation and to the strategic information we receive, we possess a greater portion of our inheritance. Therefore, as God manifests Himself through visitation, He is *shamaring* His purposes for our lives, and securing our inheritance.

5. Visitation produces glory! When the true manifest presence of God visits us as humans, His glory radiates from that presence. At times God does visibly reveal His glory, much as He did for me that night in Houston. Such a display of His presence is often seen as fire or dazzling light, perhaps as a cloud or mist, or sometimes as an act of His mighty power. But even when we do not visibly see manifestations of God's glory, the visitation leaves us with an impression of His glory burned into our hearts. It is the inward and hidden work in our hearts that produces the Christlike attributes that move us from glory to glory.

WILL GOD VISIT YOU?

Visitation can come in many different ways. God can speak directly or indirectly. You may have a strong impression that you simply know is from the Lord. You may receive a prophetic word in a time of ministry. A conversation you have with someone may give you new revelation. You may have a vivid dream that is somehow more than a subconscious response to sleep. You may read a verse of Scripture that leaps off the page and begins to stir in your spirit, as though it was written directly to you. You may be reminded of something God revealed to you some time ago that suddenly rejuvenates your faith.

When this happens you begin to experience a new realm of God's glory and manifest presence. From that, you have a new revelation of God. He is glory, and His presence causes the atmosphere around you to begin to change. It is like experiencing a little bit of heaven. I like what Ruth Ward Heflin has to say:

When glory comes down, it's a bit of Heaven's atmosphere coming down to us, a taste of His manifest presence. We don't see the air, do we? But all of us would be dead if we were not breathing it. We are not conscious of the air unless we see the wind blowing the leaves on the trees. Yet, the earth is covered by it. In the same way, not one inch of Heaven lacks glory.[4]

If none of this has happened to you and you feel you have never had a visitation from God, here is something to think about: Only God can illuminate the truth of salvation and the gospel of Jesus Christ. Therefore, if you have had a salvation experience and know Jesus as your Lord and Savior, you have had a visitation whether or not you understood it at the time! That's how simple it is. But that may not have been your only visitation. You know visitation has come when something suddenly changes the direction of your life, and God's hand was clearly in it. The truth is, God longs to visit you in a meaningful way.

The problem is that the majority of us do not understand what God wants to accomplish in our lives. So many of us walk around aimlessly with the belief that either God does not speak to individuals today, or that He is not interested enough in our specific situations to speak to us. We live day-in and day-out knowing God is watching, but perhaps never understanding that He desires active participation and interaction with us.

Sadly, multitudes of Christians never fully enter into all God has for them because they do not understand God's desire to communicate His heart directly to them. If it has been a long time since you have had a visitation, or perhaps you have never recognized God's visitations in your life, take some time to meditate on the Lord. Be quiet and still, allowing His dew of refreshing to fall on you. Ask Him for a clear word. Be open to how He might want to communicate with you. Don't ask just once, either. Be persistent until you know you have heard from the Lord.

We must position ourselves in such a way that we can hear from Him when He is ready to communicate. Your answer may not come within a few minutes or even a few days, but keep expecting. God will speak to you in some form or other. When you feel you have heard from God, write it down. Pray about it. Let it build your faith for what God longs to do for you. But don't, by any means, assume that God does not or cannot communicate with you. Being sensitive to the Holy Spirit's ability to speak into your life is a key for moving from glory to glory.

OUT OF BABYLON

When God does speak, we must realize that we have an enemy who immediately tries to steal from us what is rightfully ours. Satan will always attempt to thwart what God is doing. Such was the case for the Israelites. When they were coming out of their captivity in Babylon, they received a visitation from the Lord (see Jer. 29:10). The Israelites knew God's will for them was to return and to rebuild the destroyed Temple of the Lord. They had clearly heard from God.

God was not just being selfish in wanting His own house rebuilt. Rebuilding had a direct effect on restoring to the Israelites what had been lost in their captivity in Babylon. It was important. But as they began working toward the restoration God had for them, the enemy resisted their efforts. Instead of fighting for what they knew they were to do, the children of Israel gave in. As the people allowed the enemy to take a foothold, three things began to happen:

1. They fell into *discouragement*. They began to ask why God was calling them to rebuild the Temple in the first place.
2. Then they fell into *disillusionment*. Things weren't going well, so they began to wonder if God had really told them to build at all.

3. Finally they fell into *disinterest*. As the situation progressed, they decided they would build their own houses and leave His in disrepair. They stopped caring.

This progression of events is often a pattern for what can happen in our own lives if we do not guard what the Lord has told us and seriously pursue His will. It takes an act of our own will to choose God's plan for possessing our inheritance. In the case of the children of Israel, God used a great shaking to break discouragement, disillusionment and disinterest from them. This shaking was prophesied in Haggai 2:21. God remembered His covenant with the Israelites and continued to pursue their restoration, even when they did not. He did not shake them because of His anger, but because He wanted the glory of the latter Temple to be greater than the former. He wanted them to experience the greater glory (see Hag. 2:9).

Many times we are captured by the world around us, which attempts to hold us from the destiny God has for us. But God has a perfect time of visitation to break us out of captivity. As we respond to God, He will visit us and release us from our captivity.

Yet God will continue to pursue our restoration, even when we have come to the point of disinterest. The reason? He has a covenant with us. In the next chapter, we will take a closer look at the subject of covenant to help us understand where it fits in with all that we have studied to this point. We will also look at the process and disciplines needed to continue moving us from glory to glory.

Notes

1. Jack Hayford, *Glory on Your House* (Grand Rapids, Mich.: Chosen Books, 1991), pp. 22-23.
2. Ibid., pp. 14-18.
3. Wesley Campbell, *Welcoming a Visitation of the Holy Spirit* (Lake Mary, Fla.: Creation House, 1996), p. 60.
4. Ruth Ward Heflin, *Glory, Experiencing the Atmosphere of Heaven* (Hagerstown, Md.: The McDougal Publishing Company, 1990), p. 133.

FIVE

UNDERSTANDING GOD'S COVENANT PLAN

*"And I will establish My covenant between Me and you
and your descendants after you in their generations,
for an everlasting covenant, to be God to you and your
descendants after you."*

—GENESIS 17:7

God has a covenant with us. Not just an abstract promise of eternal life, but a personal, real covenant that ties into every one of our lives. Covenant is God's plan of agreement for His people to obtain His destined blessings. In order for us to fully possess the inheritance God has for us, we must understand what our covenant with Him is and how to come into agreement with that covenant.

WHAT IS COVENANT?

Covenant is an endless partnership or solemn and binding agreement between two or more parties. Covenant with God provides a commitment to a relationship that allows His purpose for us to be fulfilled. In their book *The Covenants*, Kevin Conner and Ken Malmin define covenant this way:

> The word "covenant" is a word that has lost its meaning and significance in present society. In Bible times, the word "covenant" involved promise, commitment, faithfulness and loyalty even unto death. A covenant was sacred and was not lightly entered into by the parties involved. In Bible times, a person was only as good as their covenant word. In a society where national agreements, business contracts, and marriage covenants are under stress and attack, where people are "covenant-breakers" (Romans 1:31), it brings great joy and comfort to know that God is a covenant-making and covenant-keeping God.[1]

WHERE DOES COVENANT COME FROM?

Covenant with God is always initiated by God Himself. He establishes it. We cannot manipulate God in this respect. We cannot go to Him and say, "Here's our proposal...." God sets the boundaries; we are responsible to operate within those boundaries.

We can clearly see that pattern throughout the Bible. As Connor and Malmin explain, God's purpose for us is seen in creation and redemption. Before the Fall, God expressed His purpose for humanity in the form of the Edenic Covenant found in Genesis 1 and 2. The promises contain God's purpose for creating the human race, which include being made in God's image, fruitfulness, multiplicity, subduing the earth, having dominion and so forth.

When Adam and Eve broke the conditions of that covenant, their disobedience necessitated an expression of God's redemptive purpose for the human race in the form of redemptive covenants, including the Adamic (Gen. 3), the Noahic (Gen. 6–9), the Abrahamic (Gen. 12–22), the Mosaic (Exod. 19–40; Gal. 3:24), the Palestinian (Deut. 27–33), the Davidic (2 Sam. 7; Pss. 89; 132), and the New Covenant (Jer. 31:31-34; Matt. 26; Heb. 8). Then there is the Everlasting Covenant which is the most comprehensive expression of both God's creative and redemptive purposes for humanity.[2]

THE NEW COVENANT AND THE EVERLASTING COVENANT

All those who have received Jesus are partakers of the New Covenant, which promises forgiveness and remission of the penalty of sin, justification and righteousness, being born again into the family of God, assurance, sanctification to the Lord, adoption as sons and daughters of God and glorification.[3]

Through the New Covenant, we have the promise of being ushered into the Everlasting Covenant at the second coming of Christ, bringing God and humanity back into covenantal relationship, eternally. The promises of this ultimate covenant include everlasting life, immortality, an everlasting kingdom which the believer inherits, an everlasting inheritance, everlasting love, kindness and mercy, everlasting habitations, everlasting joy, everlasting strength and an everlasting name.

Additionally, overcomers can lay claim to everlasting promises, which include receiving the eternal tree of life, freedom from hurt by death, hidden manna and a white stone with a new name on it, power over the nations, ruling and reigning with Jesus over all enemies, being clothed with a white raiment of light and having their names confessed before the Father and the angels, being a pillar in the Temple of God, sitting with Jesus on His throne, and inheriting all things.[4] What amazing promises for us to grasp!

In my own life, the Lord helped me grasp these covenant promises and my own responsibility within them by reading John 14—17. Much of God's covenant relationship with us, both present and to come, is revealed in these four chapters through verses such as:

"Most assuredly, I say to you, he who believes in Me, the works that I do he will do also; and greater works than these he will do, because I go to My Father. And whatever you ask in My name, that I will do, that the Father may be glorified in the Son. If you ask anything in My name, I will do it. If you love Me, keep My commandments. And I will pray the Father, and He will give you another Helper, that He may abide with you forever" (14:12-16).

"You did not choose Me, but I chose you and appointed you that you should go and bear fruit, and that your fruit should remain, that whatever you ask the Father in My name He may give you" (15:16).

"These things I have spoken to you, that in Me you may have peace. In the world you will have tribulation; but be of good cheer, I have overcome the world" (16:33).

"And for their sakes I sanctify Myself, that they also may be sanctified by the truth" (17:19).

Those who earnestly desire to understand God's covenant with us as believers should carefully study John 14—17 and allow the Spirit of God to reveal His awesome promises and purposes through this beautiful passage.

A COVENANT-KEEPING GOD

"Therefore know that the Lord your God, He is God, the faithful God who keeps covenant and mercy for a thousand generations with those who love Him and keep His commandments" (Deut. 7:9). God does not break His promises.

Once He has entered into a covenant, His faithfulness is a sure thing. Consider God's tireless display of covenant keeping to David in the following quote from Bob Beckett's book *Commitment to Conquer*:

> [God] honored David, for example, in the generations that followed that beloved king because David was a man after God's own heart. Here are two of the promises God gave David:
>
> "When your days are fulfilled and you rest with your fathers, I will set up your seed after you, who will come from your body, and I will establish his kingdom. He shall build a house for My name, and I will establish the throne of his kingdom forever" (2 Sam. 7:12,13).
>
> Not long afterward, David's son Solomon disobeyed God by taking foreign women as wives and then worshiping their gods. God was angry and intended to tear Solomon's kingdom apart. But He said, "Nevertheless I will not do it in your days, for the sake of your father David" (1 Kings 11:12).
>
> Two generations later we see David's grandson Abijam spared:
>
> And he walked in all the sins of his father, which he had done before him; his heart was not loyal to the LORD his God, as was the heart of his father David. Nevertheless for David's sake the LORD his God gave him a lamp in Jerusalem, by setting up his son after him and by establishing Jerusalem; because David did what was right in the eyes of the LORD, and had not turned aside from anything that He commanded him all the days of his life, except in the matter of Uriah the Hittite (1 Kings 15:3-5).
>
> Then, 156 years after David's death, Judah was spared because David's great-grandchildren were living in the land: "The Lord would not destroy Judah, for the sake of his servant David, as He promised him to give a lamp to him and his sons forever" (2 Kings 8:19). Finally, a full 313 years later, Jerusalem was spared once again: "For I will

defend this city, to save it for My own sake and for My servant David's sake" (2 Kings 19:34).[5]

In fact, if we were to go one step further with this covenant, we would see that God promised to establish the throne of David's kingdom forever through his son, Solomon. Jesus was, in fact, a descendant of David's through Solomon's line (see Matt. 1:6). David's throne, therefore, found its ultimate fulfillment in Jesus, who is called the Son of David, and of His kingdom there shall be no end! God is a faithful, covenant-keeping God!

COVENANT WITH NOAH

Genesis 6:18 records the first time the word "covenant" is used in the Bible. God forged a covenant with Noah that has affected all generations since. The people of his day had strayed so deeply into sin and away from God's plan for the earth that God finally had to supernaturally start over by releasing a new agreement with the earth. He released that new agreement through Noah, a man He knew He could trust with His plan.

Noah's very name meant "rest," which was prophetic of the rest God wanted to bring from the sin and consequent curse that was so prevalent in those days. Noah was dedicated to the Lord; so when the Lord spoke to him, Noah began the process of restoring the earth back into relationship with a holy God.

In Genesis 9:8-11, God gave a covenantal promise that a flood would never again destroy the whole earth. Then He gave the rainbow as a sign to remind people of His power so that when they saw it, they would remember His agreement with the earth.

A PERSONAL COVENANT

The Everlasting Covenant is meant to bring all those who have come to a saving knowledge of Christ into their eternal destiny.

This covenant provides tremendous promises that do give us a hope for our eternal future. But what about this life? The New Covenant promises address issues for this life as well as eternity.

God has a destiny for each of His children to fulfill in this lifetime. Therefore, He is longing to make covenant with each one of us in order to facilitate that destiny.

Jeremiah 29:11-13 says, *"For I know the thoughts that I think toward you, says the Lord, thoughts of peace and not of evil, to give you a future and a hope. Then you will call upon Me and go and pray to Me, and I will listen to you. And you will seek Me and find Me, when you search for Me with all your heart."*

God yearns to give us a future and a hope. He has appropriated these things for every believer. But we, too, have a part to play in receiving them. Here in Jeremiah He says that when we call upon Him, He will listen, and when we search for Him with all our hearts, we will find Him.

We must discover God's covenant plan for our personal lives. The only way to do that is to listen, to search for Him with all our hearts and to obey His commandments.

A SPIRITUAL PROTECTION—IF...

His purpose for making covenant is to bless us. It is to move us into the destiny He has for us. The covenants He makes with us offer blessings of our inheritance, both here on earth and eternally.

Covenants have tremendous spiritual implications. The purpose for making a covenant is to give a personal commitment, not only to the other party involved, but also as a declaration to those outside the covenant. For example, in a marriage relationship, the wedding ring is a symbol of that covenant. Besides being a constant reminder to each party of the covenant agreement, it also says to the rest of the world that a marriage covenant is in place, so the person is not available to enter into other romantic or sexual relationships.

Likewise, when we enter into covenant relationship with God through the blood of Jesus Christ, demonic forces know that we are covered by that blood. The blood of Jesus says to the enemy, "Hands off! This is not your territory!"

Why, then, does the enemy seem to be able to steal away the inheritance of so many Christians? Why do so many Christians walk in defeat rather than victory, never reaching their full potential or destiny? It is because we have either not understood God's covenant plan, or have chosen to live in disobedience to that covenant.

Just as in marriage, people with adultery in their hearts may find that a wedding ring actually makes someone else's spouse more attractive to them. They may pursue someone else's husband or wife with the intent of drawing that spouse into an adulterous affair. The spouse, at that point, must decide whether or not he or she will remain faithful to the marriage agreement. If the spouse does not remain faithful, that person runs a risk of losing all the covenantal elements of the marriage, and perhaps the marriage itself because of his or her indiscretion.

COVENANT-BREAKING SPIRITS

In the spiritual realm, demonic forces are like the person trying to lure a spouse away from fidelity. The mission of the covenant-breaking spirit is to be an agent of Satan's quest to kill, steal and destroy. Unless we come into full agreement with God's covenant plan for our lives, we are open targets, whether we know it or not, for these demonic forces to lure us into breaking away from our covenant with God. Once we have broken that covenant, we have stepped away from the blessings it provides.

Here's an example: A major part of our covenant with God is that we will have no other gods before Him (see Exod. 20:3). This is the first of the Ten Commandments, and God takes it very seriously. The commandment did not fall out of existence when Christ died for us. In fact, He reiterated the commandment by saying, *"You shall love the Lord your God with all your heart, with all your soul, and with all your mind. This is the first and great commandment"* (Matt. 22:37,38).

Demonic forces, however, are assigned to do nothing but try to hook us into sin or idolatry. If we have a sin in our lives that we are unwilling to give up, or hold before the Lord with an open hand, saying, "Lord, do with this what You will," we ascribe to that thing a higher value than God. We have then broken this commandment and with it have compromised our covenant.

Whenever we compromise our covenant with God, we step away from the protection and blessings of that covenant. Without that protection, Satan is free to steal from us what God had intended to be part of our inheritance! We can even kick and scream at the devil, telling him in Jesus' name to give us back sevenfold what we have lost. But until we repent before God and return to our place of right standing within His covenant, our protection against such thievery is gone. Satan can and does steal our inheritance and even our destiny when we have moved away from our covenant with God.

Covenant-breaking spirits can also cause us to break covenant with one another, which can cause reproaches to come into our lives, and even over the land we live on. David learned this lesson the hard way. *"Now there was a famine in the days of David for three years, year after year; and David inquired of the Lord. And the Lord answered, 'It is because of Saul and his bloodthirsty house, because he killed the Gibeonites'"* (2 Sam. 21:1).

What does this have to do with covenant breaking? The Gibeonites, whom Saul had killed, were a people who had entered into a covenant with Israel during Joshua's days, guaranteeing their safety. When Saul killed them, he broke that covenant agreement. As a result, a famine came upon the land and appropriate repentance had to occur in order to restore the land.

Covenant breaking is a serious matter with serious implications, especially when we consider that we and all that affects our lives can move out from under God's protection if we break covenant with Him.

THE TOWER OF BABEL

Despite God's awesome display of power and ultimate covenant with Noah, sin continued to abound upon the earth. The people, unified by one language and a common purpose, became so troublesome to God that He was forced to scatter them in both language and geography. In his book *The Twilight Labyrinth*, George Otis, Jr. explains why God had to take such drastic measures:

> Although the Babylonians' idolatry and base ambition were deeply troubling, the focus of divine concern was apparently their unity of purpose....Sin is never tame, but when it is pursued as part of a common cause, its effects are magnified exponentially. In the case of Babel, the people's moral and physical unity had attracted great attention in the spirit world. God was distressed, not over architectural designs but over the emerging nexus between unified men and gathering demonic hosts.
>
> Put simply, demons congregate where people are. There is no reason for them to be anywhere else....Had He not intervened when He did, it is possible that the power of collective visualization would have allowed coalescing demonic forces to imperil the human race....The Lord God, who had already pledged Himself to refrain from any more mass destruction of life, elected to deal with mankind's unholy alliance through geographic and linguistic separation. Men and women would be confounded rather than consumed.[6]

Even though this new generation was embroiled in sin and seeking after demonic power rather than worshiping the Lord, God kept His covenant promise by refusing to destroy them. In fact, He began searching the earth for another man through whom He could once again establish covenant on earth. That's when God found Abram.

ABRAM'S OBEDIENCE

One of the most beautiful covenant stories in the Bible is that of Abram. God called Abram out of Ur of the Chaldeans, which is a part of Babylon, told him to leave his family and everything he had been a part of, and said, "Follow me." God was breaking Abram out of the idolatrous culture in which he lived in order to establish His covenant with Abram—a covenant through which all the families of the earth have been blessed (see Gen. 12:3).

WHEN GOD IS READY TO MAKE COVENANT WITH YOU OVER YOUR PORTION, HE ALREADY HAS THE PLAN FOR HOW YOU CAN INHERIT IT.

Reading Genesis 12 caused me to be thankful that Abram obeyed God and left Ur of the Chaldeans, because in his obedience, I have been blessed. Every time Abram obeyed God, the Lord would give him revelation of how to move forward in that covenant. God gave detailed information about what Abram was to inherit and the strategy for possessing it (see Gen. 15:7-11).

When God is ready to make covenant with you over your portion, or the call that is upon your life, He already has the plan for how you can inherit it.

HOW TO ESTABLISH DEEPER COVENANT

God does not enter into a personal covenant with us without our consent or cooperation. You entered into a covenant with God when you became a Christian. Yet God has much more for you if you are willing to enter into a deeper covenant relationship with Him. If that is your desire, then the following are three things you must do:

1. Understand your calling. If you have never understood the call of God upon your life, you cannot have an understanding of your full covenant with Him. Why did God create you? What is your purpose here on earth? These are basic human questions that God is willing to answer if you will draw apart and hear what He is saying. God knew your calling before the foundations of the earth. It is not His intention to keep that calling a secret from you and watch you flounder through life. His purpose for you is success!

The calling, however, is from God. He determines it. Therefore, in order to hear Him, you must be ready to let go of preconceived notions and expectations; you must let Him set your direction.

In my own life, the first glimpse I had of my calling was during His visitation at age 18 when the Lord spoke the words, "a call to the nations" over my life. I did not understand what "a call to the nations" meant, but I submitted to the Lord, knowing I had heard clearly from Him. By His sovereign grace, He has moved me and positioned me so I would not only understand the calling but also begin to move into it.

As I have yielded to Him, I have moved into new dimensions of my calling, which has been a lifelong process. I know that I have not yet entered into the fullness of my calling, nor am I sure what it entails, but I know that I am moving toward it in God's timing. He decides when to promote me and when to hold me back. I am fully submitted to Him in it. As a result, I can rest, knowing that I am where God has me, doing what He wants me to do, under the protection of His covenant blessings.

2. Enter into covenant with God. When God extends His hand to us, we must not hesitate to reach out and take hold of it. As we begin to establish a communication system with Him through prayer and learning to hear His voice, we will begin to understand when God is ready to move us into a deeper level of covenant with Him. In chapter 6 we will explore the disciplines needed to maintain spiritual life. Those eight disciplines help us to enter more fully into covenant with God.

3. Keep covenant. As I described earlier, many times we don't see the fulfillment of our blessings because we don't keep covenant with God. Refusing to keep covenant with Him will postpone His blessings because we have moved out from under the protection of that covenant where Satan can steal from us. Refusing to keep our covenants with others, however, can also be a huge opening to the enemy in our lives.

If you have had any covenant-breaking events in your life, including divorce, adultery, broken promises or not completing what you have started, take a moment to repent of any sin you may have committed by doing so. Then ask the Lord to break the power of any covenant-breaking spirits or mind-sets off of you and your family.

LESSONS FROM ELISHA

Second Kings 4 tells a beautiful story of God's covenant plan for a personal life. In fact, this story reveals how, through obedience and persistence, God restored the same thing twice. It is the story of the prophet Elisha's passing through Shunem. While there, Elisha came across a woman. Though the text does not give her a name, it does say that she was a notable, wealthy woman. The woman persuaded Elisha to come to her home for dinner. She saw that Elisha was a godly man so, after receiving permission from her husband, the woman fixed a room where the prophet could stay whenever he passed through Shunem. This apparently became Elisha's regular stopping spot.

On one of his regular visits, Elisha asked the woman what he could do for her in return for her kindness. When he discovered that she had no children, Elisha prophesied that she would bear a son. Through the prophecy, God revealed His personal covenant plan for her. Even though she was reluctant to believe, one year later the woman bore a son. God had restored the inheritance of a child to her.

Scripture says the child grew. Then one day after suffering a terrible headache, the boy died suddenly in his mother's arms. How could it be that this child of promise, this child of restoration, was now dead? Here we learn three lessons about how the Lord keeps covenant by bringing transformation to us.

LESSON 1: REKINDLING OUR AFFECTIONS

It was through her loss that the woman's affection and desire for her promised inheritance and her faith in God were rekindled. In Arthur W. Pink's book *Gleanings From Elisha*, he says:

> She cherished the hope that the prophet would restore her son to her. She made no preparations for the burial of the child, but anticipated his resurrection by laying him upon Elisha's bed. Her faith clung to the original blessing: God, by the prophet's promise and prayers, had given him unto her, and now she takes the dead child to God (as it were) and goes to seek the prophet.[7]

As human beings, our affections (those things that we love or have a special attachment to) are linked with our desires. If the fire of God is not in our affections, we often lack the faith we need to see our restoration and, consequently, God's plan for our lives come to fruition. Had this woman not sought out the prophet but decided to bury her son and begin her grieving, she would never have seen her child restored. But she passionately sought out the prophet, traveling what appeared to be a long and hard journey from Shunem to Carmel where Elisha was holding meetings. She pleaded with Elisha for her son's life, reminding him that this boy was a promise of God. Writing about her passion during that time, Arthur W. Pink goes on to comment:

An intense earnestness possessed the soul of this woman, and where such earnestness is joined with faith, it refuses all denial. While our faith remains a merely mental and mechanical thing, it achieves nothing; but when it is intense and fervent, it will produce results. True, it requires a deep sense of need, often the pressure of an urgent situation, to evoke this earnestness. That is why faith flourishes most in times of stress and trial, for it then has its most suitable opportunity to declare itself.[8]

Many in the Body of Christ have not allowed their affections to be rekindled by God at a time of loss. They have believed God for His promise and seen Him bring it to birth, only to watch that precious manifestation of God's love die later on. The pure heartbreak of the disappointment alone is enough to bruise our affections and expectations toward God's covenant-keeping with us. But we must remember that God needs to deal with the mind, will and emotions to make us whole.

Our affections are part of our emotions. Therefore, unless our affections are brought before God and exposed to Him, we will never truly have the desires of our hearts. As we allow even our bruised affec-

---

IF THE FIRE OF GOD IS NOT IN OUR AFFECTIONS, WE OFTEN LACK THE FAITH WE NEED TO SEE OUR RESTORATION AND, CONSEQUENTLY, GOD'S PLAN FOR OUR LIVES COME TO FRUITION.

---

tions to be rekindled by God, He will also renew our ability to believe in Him so that His covenant blessings can come forth. That is what happened to the woman in this story. Her affection for the child God had promised her sparked her faith in such a way that she believed God to restore her dead son. And God responded by doing just that!

God will always respond when we allow Him to rekindle our affections. God is not, however, obligated to respond just because we may feel intensely about an issue, or assume something to be His will. However, when we earnestly come before the Lord and lay down all of our emotions, He does bring healing to our wounds and a divine order to our desires. He will rekindle our affections, which are directly linked to our desires. That process, in turn, will directly affect our level of faith in Him.

I believe that allowing my affections to be rekindled was part of what happened to me when I was 18. Somewhere I had experienced death, lost hope and gone astray. Yet as God penetrated my being, and I allowed Him to deal with my battered emotions, I was able to begin believing in His covenant plan for my life. I desired all He had for me, and as that desire grew, it was as if a gift of faith was imparted to me. Throughout the years, I've watched God release that gift of faith, rekindle that gift of faith and stir that gift of faith at just the right moments in my life. He has never failed!

LESSON 2: DEALING WITH OUR BRAINS

In this story we see that the child died after getting a tremendous headache. Something had happened in his brain to stop it from functioning. When Elisha finally came, he laid on the lifeless child once and the boy's flesh began to warm. But it was not until Elisha laid on him the second time that the child sneezed seven times and was restored to life.

Though not immediately, God dealt with the child's brain and restored life and understanding to him. I believe God wants us to allow Him to deal with our brains in order to restore life and understanding about His plan for us. We need to take those things that have seemingly died in our lives and ask the Lord to give us specific understanding and strategy to see them renewed.

In this story, Elisha knew that reviving the boy would require laying on the child, mouth-to-mouth, eye-to-eye, and hand-to-hand. That was the strategy. Yet the first time Elisha stretched out on the boy, he was not fully restored. His flesh warmed, but he was still lifeless. Elisha walked back and forth in the house, and then went back to stretch out on the child once more. Only then did God work a miracle of resurrection. It took both an understanding of the strategy and the faith to persist in that strategy until the child was fully alive again.

A principle of covenant is understanding. We need to know what God wants to do in our lives and what part we play in seeing that plan come to fruition. Ask God for knowledge and understanding. Knowledge does not puff us up. Knowledge gives us pieces so we can begin to put together the strategy for possessing our inheritance.

LESSON 3: RELEASING NEW VISION
After the young boy sneezed seven times, he was restored to life. Then he opened his eyes. He could see again—not just the room in which he lay, but he could also see that life had been restored to him. Vision for his whole future opened before his eyes. It would not be a stretch of the imagination to assume that neither the young boy nor his mother would ever see his life in the same way after that incident. The very hand of God had moved on his behalf! Even though the Scriptures do not say it as such, I would not doubt that both the mother and boy felt a certain sense of destiny for him from that point on.

The Lord wants you to look at those things in your life that seem dead and fruitless. Look at those things over which you have no vision or have lost your vision. Ask Him to bring resurrection life back into those dead places and renew your vision for your own destiny.

HOW THE SHUNAMMITE'S DEEPER COVENANT WAS ESTABLISHED

Earlier in this chapter we discussed three things you must do to establish a deeper covenant with God. Throughout this story we can see how the Shunammite woman was faithful to all three of those things, and how she then entered into God's covenant plan.

1. She understood her calling. Because of her wealth and her husband's willingness, the Shunammite woman was able to make a "prophet's chamber" for Elisha. She expected nothing in return for her kind hospitality, except that she be privileged enough to host a man of God. Yet, this was her calling. This was what God required of her and she was faithful in it. As a result, the covenant blessings of God were showered upon her.

2. She entered into covenant with God. This woman was open to hear the voice of the prophet who spoke into her life. Though she had some trouble believing the prophet at first, she still entered into agreement with what he said, knowing that God was fully able to lift her barrenness and cause her to conceive her promised son.

3. She kept covenant with God. Even when it seemed that all was lost and her son was suddenly dead, the Shunammite woman would not let go of the promise God had given her. She did not retreat from God—she pressed into Him with greater faith. Had she prepared her son for burial and began to mourn his death, she might never have moved forward in her covenant plan; it could have ended then and there. But her persistence and faith were the evidence of a powerful act of her own covenant-keeping, and God responded by restoring life to her son!

BUT, THERE'S MORE!

The raising of this child is not the end of this woman's story in the Bible. In 2 Kings 8, we read about her again. In this passage, Elisha predicts seven years of famine and warned her about the impending curse. The woman then left her house and land behind to go to the land of the Philistines where her family was protected from the famine.

At the end of those seven years, she returned home. The house and land which the woman once owned were no longer hers because she had abandoned them. So, she made an appeal to the king, asking him to have her possessions restored. At that same time, the king had been asking Elisha's servant to tell him of the great things God had done through the prophet. The servant had, apparently, just been telling him of bringing the boy back to life when the woman and the boy showed up.

Greatly impressed, the king asked the woman to recount the miracle, which she did. As a result, the king not only restored her house and land, but gave her all the proceeds of the field for the seven years she had been gone!

God's rich blessings were not limited to the day her son was raised from the dead. Because she testified to His miraculous works in her life, she received an abundant blessing beyond what she even asked for years later. God's faithfulness to His covenant promises never ends!

Notes

1. Kevin Conner and Ken Malmin, *The Covenants* (Portland, Oreg.: Bible Temple Publishing, 1983), Foreword.
2. Ibid, pp. 3-4, 10-11.
3. Ibid., pp. 73-74. Scripture references cited for promises are: forgiveness and remission of the penalty of sin (Acts 10:43; 13:36-39), justification and righteousness (Rom. 5:1; 3:24-26), being born again into the family of God (Matt. 6:9; John 3:1-5; 1 Pet. 1:23), assurance (Heb. 5:8,9; 6:10-12; 10:38,39; 1 John 3:19), sanctification to the Lord (John 17:17; Eph. 5:26,27; 1 Thess. 5:23,24), adoption as sons and daughters of God (Rom. 8:15,23; Gal. 4:5; Eph. 1:13,14), and glorification (John 17:22-24; Rom. 8:17,30; 2 Cor. 3:18).
4. Ibid., pp. 95-96. Scripture references cited for promises are: everlasting life (Dan. 12:2; Matt. 19:29; Luke 18:30; John 3:16,36; 4:14; 5:24; 6:27,40,47; 12:50; Acts 13:46; Rom. 6:22; Gal. 6:8; 1 Tim. 6:16), immortality (Rom. 2:7; 1 Cor. 15:15-57; 2 Cor. 5:1-5; 1 Tim. 6:16; 2 Tim. 1:9,10), an everlasting kingdom which the believer inherits (Ps. 145:13; Dan. 4:3,34; 7:14,27; Matt. 25:34; 1 Cor. 6:9,10; Gal. 5:21; Eph. 5:5; 2 Pet. 1:11), eternal inheritance (Heb. 9:14), everlasting love, kindness and mercy (Pss. 100:5; 103:17; Isa. 54:8; Jer. 31:3), everlasting righteousness (Dan. 9:24), everlasting habitations (Luke 16:9), everlasting joy (Isa. 51:11; 61:7), everlasting strength (Isa. 26:4), and an

everlasting name (Isa. 56:5; 63:12,16). Scripture references for promises for overcomers are: being given the eternal tree of life (Rev. 2:7), not be hurt by death (Rev. 2:11), given hidden manna and a white stone with a new name in it (Rev. 2:17), power over the nations, ruling and reigning with Jesus over all enemies (Rev. 2:26-28), being clothed with white raiment of light and having his or her name confessed before the Father and the angels (Rev. 3:4,5), being a pillar in the temple of God (Rev. 3:12), sitting with Jesus on His throne (Rev. 3:21), and inheriting all things (Rev. 21:7).

5. Bob Beckett, *Commitment to Conquer* (Grand Rapids, Mich.: Chosen Books, 1997), pp. 85-86.

6. George Otis, Jr., *The Twilight Labyrinth* (Grand Rapids, Mich.: Chosen Books, 1997), pp. 117-119.

7. Arthur W. Pink, *Gleanings From Elisha* (Chicago, Ill.: Moody Press, 1972), p. 80.

8. Ibid., pp. 83-84.

THE PROCESS OF
SPIRITUAL LIFE

*Godliness is profitable for all things, having promise of
the life that now is and of that which is to come.*

—1 TIMOTHY 4:8

By now you may be asking, "What does God expect of me? What is
my part in the covenant I have with Him?" Most of that answer
is wrapped up in what Jesus called the first and great commandment:
*"Love the Lord your God with all your heart, with all your soul, and with all
your mind"* (Matt. 22:37). We are to be totally His. Only then can we
begin to possess our inheritance.

Throughout the years God has shown me a nine-step process
that helps us gain victory in our spiritual lives and helps us move
into the *zoe* life He has for each of us.

VISITATION IN THE BATHROOM!

The first four steps in this nine-step process were made clear to me one day when God met me in the bathroom for a four-hour lesson I'll never forget!

I was 24 years old. My life was going along nicely. I had been married to a beautiful woman for five years; I had become successful in the business world, working as system director of human resources for a major oil company; I taught a good Bible study—I was really enjoying the blessings of God in my life.

Then one day, out of nowhere, I was confronted by a sister in the Lord who worked for me. She brought my attention to a potential weakness she saw in my life and suggested that I was in danger of falling into gross sin if I did not deal with it. I was shocked. I can honestly say that at the time I was pure in heart, but it was something I had been totally blind to. I realized I had to give it a hard look, so I went to talk to the most spiritual person I knew, my wife Pam. As I discussed the issue with her, Pam confirmed that she too had seen that potential weakness for some time and agreed that I needed to deal with it before the Lord. In fact, Pam suggested I had a stronghold to deal with.

I didn't really know what she was talking about, but I knew I had to be with the Lord and wrestle it through. (I have since learned that a stronghold is, as Ed Silvoso defines it, "a mind-set impregnated with hopelessness that causes us to accept as unchangeable, situations that we know are contrary to the will of God."[1]) I took the Bible into the bathroom and, starting in Romans 6, read it aloud to Him.

I continued to read with uninterrupted steadiness until I came to verses 8 and 9, which say, *"Now if we died with Christ, we believe that we shall also live with Him, knowing that Christ, having been raised from the dead, dies no more. Death no longer has dominion over Him."* As I read these verses, something began to awaken within me. The truth that death no longer had dominion over me because of Christ became an absolute reality.

Then I read verses 10 to 12: *"For the death that He died, He died to sin once for all; but the life that He lives, He lives to God. Likewise you also, reckon yourselves to be dead indeed to sin, but alive to God in Christ Jesus our Lord. Therefore do not let sin reign in your mortal body, that you should obey it in its lusts."* I sensed the Lord say that if death had no dominion over me, then I was to reckon myself as dead to sin and not obey whatever urges might come up.

It went on. Verse 13: *"And do not present your members as instruments of unrighteousness to sin, but present yourselves to God as being alive from the dead, and your members as instruments of righteousness to God."* I did not know how to do this, so I simply rose to my feet and said out loud, "Lord, I present myself alive from the dead to You." As I did this, I actually presented each member of my body to the Lord for sanctification.

Then verse 14: *"For sin shall not have dominion over you, for you are not under law but under grace."* Suddenly I saw the power of sin that was working. I saw that God had made provision so sin would not have dominion over me. I asked the Lord, "Is this really true?" and as clearly as I have ever heard any voice, the Lord said, "Yes." Then I asked Him if the rest of the Bible and everything He had promised in it was true, and He said, "Yes, obey it." God began to awaken great faith in me that all His Word was true. I read other Scriptures, stopping in certain places that had been hard to believe, asking God if this or that was true. He always answered, "Yes."

Throughout that process, God's manifest presence—His glory—filled that bathroom. Four hours later when I came out, my wife could hardly recognize me. My whole countenance was different; it was softer. It was as though God had taken a chisel and began to break away hard places that had been holding me back. Those places included insecurities, rejection, lust and the power that had caused previous generations in my family to turn away from God. As He broke through those hard places, He began to release new dimensions of Himself into me. I had a whole new understanding of the Bible. I had a whole new faith. I was on the road to victory in my spiritual life!

A NINE-STEP PROCESS

The Lord has promised us abundant life. The following are nine steps that will help you move into a new level of spiritual or *zoe* life:

1. Submit to God. If we were to be honest, most of us would have to admit that we cringe at the thought of submission. Yet submission is the first step toward possessing our inheritance in the Lord. We can't skip it and go on to step 2. In an effort to understand what submission is and is not, here is a helpful truth from Jack Hayford's book *The Power and Blessing*:

> Perhaps few words have suffered at the hands of human misapplication more than "submission." The word is doubly abused, having been rendered the equivalent of "patsy" or "wimp" if a person chooses to be "submitted." And submission has also mistakenly been made synonymous with "subjugation." But "to submit" is neither to become somebody's doormat, nor is submission the enforced requirement of a conqueror or tyrant.
>
> The Word of God has a great deal to say about a disciple's learning "submission," but it never suggests that to do so is to resign human dignity, intelligence, or good sense. To the contrary, God is the author of true human dignity (which is the opposite of pride, the fallen man's substitute), and the God-given human capacities of intelligence and good sense are never denigrated by Him (though faith will often overreach both while denying the practical value of neither).
>
> Submission has to do with our sensible acceptance of our appropriate place in God's order of things. It has everything to do with clear-headed thinking and nothing to do with empty-headed self-centeredness.[2]

Pastor and author Palma Chandler suggests that submitting is synonymous with believing. He writes:

> The word "submit" means to yield or surrender to the authority of another. God's Word is His manifested authority. Having faith in God is: (1) taking God at His Word; and (2) trusting God to bring His Word to pass. The term "believe" is an action word. It carries with it the idea of corresponding actions. Therefore, when I submit to God, I surrender to the authority of His Word. This causes me, my life, and my circumstances to line up with what He wills, which is what He says.[3]

To submit is to make a decision based on trust, to get in your right place. It's that simple. Our right place is to be in obedience to God, doing His will. When I realized that I was in spiritual trouble, I went into the bathroom that day to hear what God had to say. In the process of not simply denying that any sin could be working in my life but rather going to God, I submitted to Him. I got in my right place before Him. It was in that place of submission that I was able to hear Him clearly and move to the next step.

2. Resist the devil, the author of sin. Satan does have the right to tempt us, but we have the authority to withstand his temptations. During my time in the bathroom, God was faithful to show me that sin had no right to dwell in me—at any level. He also showed me that I had the power to resist temptation. By reckoning myself dead to sin and not obeying its lusts, I could just say no. I could walk away, not only from present temptations, but from those to which I could have been vulnerable.

We have the power to resist sin. Romans 6:14 says that sin does not have dominion over us. It does not rule our lives. Sometimes, however, special warfare is required to break the power sin may have over us. This step is essential to moving forward. If we do not resist the power of sin, how can we resist Satan when he comes to steal what is ours? Our sin gives him a right to be there!

3. Draw near to God. While in the bathroom, I did not know how to present myself to God as being alive from the dead. Thus I simply did what I thought it might mean by verbalizing my desire to do so. As I did, I drew near to Him in the best way I knew how at the time. Then, just as James 4:8 promises, He drew near to me by allowing His sweet and awesome presence to fill the room.

It is not necessary to have a manifested glory, or to hear an audible voice, in order to experience the presence of God. And yet every time we make an effort to draw near to Him, something is deposited in our spirits even if we are not consciously aware of it. Draw near to Him, and He will draw near to you!

4. Gain revelation. As I drew near to God, and He drew near to me, I was able to begin asking questions about Scriptures that puzzled me. The profound revelation that I gained that day was that God's Word was true—every bit of it. That revelation may not seem like much. After all, God's Word is truth. Nonetheless, there were certain points over which I was skeptical. Since that visitation, however, I have had a level of faith in my spiritual life that has seen me through many years.

ONCE GOD HAS REVEALED THAT SOMETHING IS ABSOLUTELY TRUE, NO FURTHER QUESTION REMAINS. IT'S AS IF A VEIL IS RIPPED FROM YOUR EYES, AND HAVING SEEN THE TRUTH, NOTHING CAN MAKE YOU GO BACK.

But the assurance about His Word was not the only revelation I had that day. I began to understand detailed steps for overcoming sin and darkness in my life. I began to understand how to walk into new levels of spiritual life that have produced the steps I'm describing here. A whole new dimension of my relationship with God was born that day. The Word of God became alive within me, and it opened up a path of communication with God that remains to this day.

Revelation will do that for anyone. Once God has revealed that something is absolutely true, no further question remains. It's as if a veil is ripped from your eyes, and having seen the truth, nothing can cause you to back up. All revelation that brings victory in our lives comes only from God. Therefore, in order to overcome the enemy on any level, we must seek God to gain revelation.

5. Define your vision. Earlier we talked about understanding the calling God has placed on your life. Understanding your call is directly linked to gaining your vision because your calling produces your vision—both what you are called to be and what you are called to accomplish. If this is not defined, you have no direction and cannot know what God's destiny is for you.

Proverbs 29:18 says, *"Where there is no vision [no redemptive revelation of God], the people perish" (Amp.).* People who do not receive God's revelation to propel themselves forward in their lives, actually begin to decline. As human beings, we are either in a state of growing or diminishing. Therefore, in order to continue growing, we need to be reaching toward something. For that we need vision.

But gaining vision does not necessarily have to be an overwhelming process. In John P. Kotter's secular book *Leading Change*, he says:

> The word vision connotes something grand or mystical, but the direction that guides successful transformations is often simple and mundane....A vision can be mundane and simple, at least partially, because in successful transformations, it is only one element in a larger system that also includes strategies, plans and budgets...without a good vision, a clever strategy or a logical plan rarely can [we] inspire the kind of action needed to produce major change.[4]

Remember, our vision is linked with our calling. If you feel you have not defined the vision God has for you in this season of your life, ask Him to clarify your call. Out of that call, allow Him to define your vision and show you the direction you are to take.

6. Develop strategy. Once you begin to understand your vision, you need to allow God to show you the strategy for getting from point A to point B. Strategy occurs when we set forth the plan to advance. Spiritually, that plan will have to meet the enemy's opposition. Vision sets the overall; strategy establishes the steps for reaching that goal.

In Ephesians 6, Paul tells those he addresses to stand against the schemes and the wiles of Satan who is trying to stop them from reaching their destiny. The enemy has schemes and strategies to stop you. But God has a higher strategy for His people to reach their goals which the enemy cannot even attain. Strategy causes you to reach the goal that God has asked you to reach.

I find that many pastors can get bogged down in this aspect of reaching their goals because they think if they have the right revelation and know the will of God and are preaching it to the people, the people will automatically walk in it. That, unfortunately, is not so. Leaders need strategies to see that every person in the congregation (children, youth, adults) can be equipped to understand and act on what God is calling them to accomplish. Then, they have to look out into the community to see how to meet the needs.

7. Acquire provision. *"And my God shall supply all your need according to His riches in glory by Christ Jesus"* (Phil. 4:19). As we move in our strategies, provision is released. God will always supply all your needs based on the vision He has called you to walk in. The Lord has all the resources necessary to accomplish the vision and carry out the strategy He has set for you. Many times, though, the enemy is there to block that vision, and one of his favorite methods for doing so is to cut off supply.

However, the word "provision" means to prepare to meet a need—to have it already stored up. God's vision and strategy carries with it the necessary provision; it is only a matter of bringing the revelation of release down on earth.

8. Achieve your mission. There are four things to remember while moving toward the fulfillment of your mission:

A. *You must set your face like a flint to reach your goal. God has a "there" for you.* Once provision is flowing with vision and strategy and you know where your "there" is, you must begin to set your face toward accomplishing your mission. Luke 9:51 says that when the time had come for Jesus to go to Jerusalem to be crucified, He set His face steadfastly (or like a flint) to reach Jerusalem. He knew His next "there," and nothing could have stopped Him.

B. *You must recognize the authority of God.* In Matthew 8, we find Jesus and the disciples in a boat when a fierce storm hits. Jesus is peacefully asleep in the bottom of the boat. But the disciples forget that Jesus is with them in their journey to the next "there" and fear overtakes them. At the disciples' insistence, Jesus gets up and demonstrates His authority by rebuking the elements. Many times we do not reach our "there" because of the tumultuous circumstances that come against us. The Lord always has the authority to overthrow that which would keep us from coming into our next "there." As we recognize the authority of God, we can begin to overcome the fears that hit us as a storm rages around us.

C. *You must be willing to address and confront those things that would keep you from coming into your place.* We tend to thrive on formulas. It's easier to get a formula for success than to seek God daily to discover His plan of victory for us. But we must take the time to pray and seek God. Discernment in this process is an important factor. You must know whether the elements or circumstances you are facing are from the enemy, who is trying to get you off course, or from God, who is attempting to switch your course. If it is the enemy, then ask the Lord for a strategy to wage warfare against his schemes. If it is the Lord, then adjust what needs to be adjusted and continue toward your "there."

    D. *You must get to the "there" that God has for you.* God has a way to get you to your next place in His perfect will for your life. Trust Him to get you "there."

You will find that as you follow these steps, God will help you achieve your mission and get to your next "there."

9. Secure your covenant blessings and purposes. When the mission is accomplished, then the Lord calls us to secure (fasten, affix, bring into safety) those blessings that He has for us as we reach our "there." We must secure the perimeters of our new place, and all the blessings the Lord has for us.

In his book *That None Should Perish*, Ed Silvoso writes:

> Success depends on a secure perimeter. We must secure the perimeter against the devil and his schemes. This is an act of war. Satan's preferred mode of operation is exploiting ignorance, our ignorance, because it allows him to move with impunity.[5]

Silvoso then goes on to list the three main weapons Satan uses to keep us from securing our perimeter: sin, accusation and strongholds of the mind, all of which we will discuss later.[6] We do need to recognize that securing our perimeter is, in fact, an act of war, and we must be willing to enter into that war if we are to establish our place in our new "there."

DISCIPLINES FOR MAINTAINING SPIRITUAL LIFE

Now that we have looked at the steps to discovering a new level of *zoe* life, we need to understand the disciplines involved in maintaining it. The following are eight key maintenance disciplines that will also prevent the enemy from stealing your inheritance and keep the "spiritual life" process flowing. As you read through these eight points, ask God to give you a plan to develop any disciplines in which you may be weak.

1. Meditation. *"This Book of the Law shall not depart from your mouth, but you shall meditate in it day and night, that you may observe to do according to all that is written in it. For then you will make your way prosperous, and then you will have good success"* (Josh. 1:8).

One of the ways God has provided for our success is contingent upon our willingness to take time to meditate on His Word. Why? Because if we just read God's Word without taking the time to give it thought, we deny ourselves the opportunity to receive personal revelation, refreshment for our souls and spirits, and increased understanding in order to align ourselves with His will in prayer.

Pastor and author Donald S. Whitney puts it this way:

Meditation is the missing link between Bible intake and prayer....There should be a smooth, almost unnoticeable transition between Scripture input and prayer output so that we move even closer to God in those moments. This happens when there is the link of meditation in between.[7]

Meditation is actually synonymous with a cow chewing its cud. The cow will eat some food and then later bring it back up and chew on it again and again until the food finally becomes part of that cow's being. Many times when God speaks to us, we are in awe and have no clue how God will accomplish what He spoke. Mary pondered (meditated on) what the Holy Spirit spoke to her about the birth of Jesus. It became a part of her until she brought it to birth and watched it grow to maturity and into the fullness of God's plan. We need to be like Mary and allow God's Word to become a part of us.

The problem is simply a matter of patience. I have found that, as a whole, our society is very impatient. Add to that the nonstop hectic schedules most people face, and there seems little time for quality meditation. We must repent before God for not following the command to meditate day and night, and ask Him to break the power of impatience from us. Once that happens, and we learn the discipline of meditation, we will find that we are willing to wait on God until we hear from Him concerning our circumstances.

2. Prayer. My life is a life of prayer. I would rather commune with God than with anyone else. Prayer is very simply communication with God. We will never advance in any aspect of our Christian lives without prayer, whether they are prayers of thanksgiving, repentance, supplication or intercession on someone else's behalf. The great people and role models of the Bible were those who sought God and found out what He would have them accomplish on this earth.

We are commanded in God's Word to devote ourselves to prayer (see Col. 4:2) and to pray continually (see 1 Thess. 5:17). We simply cannot cultivate our relationship with God through substitutes. Love is evidenced through relationship and relationship is evidenced through communication; therefore, the depth of our relationship with Him can only grow as we spend time communicating with Him. We cannot know what our destiny is, what our portion is, or what He intended for us without the discipline of prayer. We cannot understand or honor our covenant with Him apart from prayer. When we pray, the channels to God open—both ways. To neglect prayer is to neglect God Himself.

3. Fasting. Fasting is a discipline that most religions and cults understand because this sacrifice releases power.

For the Christian, fasting is essential. Often you cannot gain the revelation you need for your next step without it. Even Jesus agreed that some things simply could not be accomplished without fasting. Fasting, unlike baptism, communion or observing the Sabbath, is not an end in itself. It is a means to an end, which is a complete separating to God. Fasting removes spiritual clutter and positions us to receive from God. By fasting, we make it possible for the Lord to more powerfully reveal Himself to us—not because He speaks more clearly when we fast, but because we can hear Him more clearly.

Why? Because we have given up something temporal in order to pursue something eternal. The degree to which we allow ourselves to hunger after God is the degree to which we will be satisfied by Him.

Isaiah 58, the great chapter on fasting, offers us a list of additional benefits that fasting can produce, including deliverance, giving, guidance, healing, increased protection, spiritual cleansing, answers from God, increased fruitfulness and restoration of spiritual things that have been lost. Even so, fasting is not a magical ritual to manipulate God. Fasting is a sacrifice of submission and worship unto Him, and the fruit it will produce is His to decide. Yet fasting not in legalism or religious duty, but by obedience to the God with whom you have a personal relationship—will produce a deeper covenant relationship with Him.[8]

4. Giving. Giving is a real key in my own life. I believe giving is the very heart of God. Giving is linked with worship, and we must recognize that the Son of Righteousness really can't arise within us if we are not giving God His portion. Therefore, we cannot come into our inheritance if we are unwilling to honor Him with what is rightfully His. Remember, the Lord says in His Word that the first 10 percent *belongs* to Him. We cannot come into our portion if we rob Him of His portion (see Mal. 3:8). Tithing is a part of our covenant with Him. Once we have tithed the first 10 percent, He allows us to be a steward of the other 90 percent. And what we do with that other 90 percent does affect how we see our portion multiplied.

In the parable of the talents (see Matt. 25), we find that judgment came on the servant who merely buried his portion without trying to multiply it. And we, too, are called to multiply what God has given us. But there is no way we can do that without giving—it's the law of sowing and reaping. We cannot reap (or multiply) that which we are not willing to sow (or give).

Often, however, we operate in a lack or poverty mentality. We can easily forget that everything we have God created and gave to us. Jack Hayford says, "Poverty is more than not having something. It's a spirit that is always *fearful* of not having anything at all."9 We must overcome our fear of lack that may be keeping us from giving and allow God to lead us into freedom in this whole issue.

5. Warfare. Like it or not, we are in a war that began the day we got saved. On that day we were taken from the kingdom of darkness into the Kingdom of light. Those two kingdoms are violently opposed to each other. Anything that God has ordained us to accomplish is going to be met with resistance from our enemy. Therefore, Satan has set himself against God's destiny for us.

In order to reach our full potential in God, we must learn warfare. Sometimes, however, warfare is not as aggressive as it sounds. For example, every one of these eight disciplines is a form of warfare because each one thwarts the enemy's plans to steal God's best from us. Keeping covenant with God is a powerful form of warfare; it sets up a protection around us that cannot be easily penetrated by demonic forces. Tithing our income is a form of warfare because it brings God's blessings on our finances and shuts out Satan's curses. Repentance is one of the strongest forms of warfare because it removes Satan's legal right in a situation.

At times, however, we must enter into warfare prayer. Therefore, when we are in an intimate place with the Lord, He will begin to give us the strategy we need to defeat the enemy in whatever battles we face. Personally, I don't war just to war. God has set me in His abiding place (see Ps. 91). When the enemy tries to prevent me from getting into or pulling me out of my abiding place, then he and I go to war.

6. Worship. Worship, both corporate and private, is a key discipline to maintaining spiritual life. Worship is that place where we can come into intimacy with God. It is not just singing songs, although music can be a catalyst for expressing deep worship to the Lord. Worship is a lifestyle of focusing our minds and hearts on

God and all that He is. It is a response to all He has done for us. It is a fragrant, flowering offshoot of our covenant relationship with Him.

Many, many things in life are worship issues. In fact, every discipline we have mentioned can be an act of worship, because these disciplines give reverence and honor to God and can bring intimacy with Him.

In my own life, I believe that worship paved the way for God to miraculously heal my wife Pam of barrenness. She and I had been trying without success to conceive children for 10 years. At the time we were in a traditional, denominational church that was unaccustomed to demonstrations of worship such as lifting hands. But God had so strongly revealed His love to me that I could not keep from raising my hands in worship to Him on a regular basis.

One night, on the way home from attending a powerful conference with outstanding worship, Pam said, "Chuck, I have never quite understood your demonstrative worship. In the New Testament there are only two places where it even talks about lifting hands."

I remember looking at her and saying, "I don't really care if it's just in the footnotes. I long to express myself to God because of His love for me. You know, you might allow yourself to express your love to Him, too."

The next day in that conference, I felt the Spirit of God envelop us with a powerful presence. I looked over at Pam. For the first time since I'd known her, Pam had both hands raised high in the air worshiping the Lord. Her face was beet red. I asked her what was happening, and she said she felt as though hot oil was being poured on her head and flowing down her body. At that very moment, while my wife worshiped the Lord, a clot dislodged itself and passed from her uterus.

Shortly after that day, Pam had her first normal cycle in years, and within one month had conceived our daughter. Since then, Pam has given birth to six children. I firmly believe that her willingness to step out of her comfort zone and worship the Lord that day was the avenue through which God miraculously healed her of barrenness! Her obedience unlocked the seed to our inheritance of children.

Without the discipline of worship, there can be many, many things that the Lord is longing to bring to birth in your life but He simply can't because the relationship you have with Him lacks the intimacy necessary to conceive those things.[10]

7. Work. I am an intercessor. I love to spend as much time as possible each day in prayer. But, God requires more than prayer. There is a time to get up off your knees and do something. We can pray all day, but eventually we have to realize that God will come to us and show us what He wants us to do. Many times we can speak to the mountain; other times we have to dig through it to get to the other side. I call that spiritual work.

God, Himself, expressed the concept of work through the six days of creation. He labored in those days to form all that came into existence.

In the book of Haggai we see that the people began to build the Temple, but eventually stopped. The Lord said to them, "Consider your ways" (1:5). Then He commanded them to go to work so that His glory could be seen in His temple.

The book of Nehemiah is all about the people rebuilding the walls of the city, which was God's command. In Nehemiah we see a picture of how work and prayer come together to accomplish God's purposes: half the people worked while the other half held the swords (see Neh. 4:16). There comes a time to roll up your sleeves and do the work that is required of you. Work is not only honorable, but is also a necessary discipline for the process of spiritual life and for seeing the fulfillment of God's covenant plan for you.

8. Rest. Though God labored six days, He rested on the seventh. In the Ten Commandments, He commanded us to do so as well. Rest must be a big issue to make the top 10! There are several reasons why this is so: First, rest is a matter of obedience to God. He has commanded us to rest. The children of Israel learned this lesson the hard way when, because of their unwillingness to observe God's Sabbath command, they were sent into captivity in Babylon.

Second, rest is an issue of trust in God. An article written by my good friend and colaborer Cindy Jacobs, says:

> *Vine's Old Testament* concordance says that by resting, man witnessed his trust in God to give fruit to his labor. Perhaps when we continue to work without time off, we are saying to God, "You cannot bless the fruit of my labor if I take time out" (or) "I have to do this even if it breaks down my physical body, or causes harm to my loved ones" (or) "There is no one but me who can do what I do." Now, most of us would state up front that we don't believe that, but our actions belie this.[11]

Third, and perhaps most obvious, is our physical well-being. God knows how He created us and how much physical rest we need. We must rest to gain the new strength needed for what lies ahead. An extra cup of coffee in the morning will *not* accomplish the same thing!

The Sabbath rest means to stop, cease or end and meditate on the glories of God's creation, which is a fourth reason to rest. In Jacobs's article, she goes on to say, "One aspect of the Sabbath was that it was to be a day or season of reflecting on God, who He is and what He has done for us in all of His fullness. This is a powerful concept. Rest is not complete without time to reflect on the Lord."[12] Such rest and reflection is what is being referred to in Psalm 23: *"He lets me rest in green meadows; he leads me beside peaceful streams"* (v. 2, *NLT*). This is a picture of stillness and meditation.

Fifth, it is from this time of quietness that we can receive revelation and strategy for moving forward toward victory. This is why the Lord told Joshua to meditate day and night on His covenant for success in taking the Promised Land. As Joshua obeyed the Lord, God gave him what he needed to move the children of Israel into their inheritance.

There is another aspect to rest, however, than that which we observe by taking a Sabbath. Spiritual rest comes when we enter into the fullness of God's plan for our provision and portion. We rest when we reach our "there" and secure our covenant blessings.

May you enter into the rest you need and receive new strength to obtain the promises over your life!

Notes

1. Ed Silvoso, *That None Should Perish* (Ventura, Calif.: Regal Books, 1994), p. 154.
2. Jack Hayford, *The Power and Blessing* (Wheaton, Ill.: Victor Books, 1994), pp. 33-34.
3. Palma Chandler, *The Miracle of True Prayer* (South Holland, Ill.: Creative Ways Multimedia, 1997), p. 125.
4. John P. Kotter, *Leading Change* (Boston, Mass.: Harvard Business School Press, 1996), p. 71.
5. Silvoso, p. 230.
6. Ibid., pp. 230-231.
7. Donald S. Whitney, *Spiritual Disciplines for the Christian Life* (Colorado Springs, Colo.: Navpress, 1991), p. 67.
8. For further study, see Elmer Towns, *Fasting for Spiritual Breakthrough* (Ventura, Calif.: Regal Books, 1996).
9. Jack Hayford, *Glory on Your House* (Grand Rapids, Mich.: Chosen Books, 1994), p. 184.
10. For further study on worship, see Joseph L. Garlington, *Worship, the Pattern of Things in Heaven* (Shippensburg, Pa.: Destiny Image, 1997).
11. Cindy Jacobs, "The Sabbath's Rest," *G.I. News* (Colorado Springs, Colo.: Generals of Intercession, 1995), Vol. 4, No. 1, January/February, p. 1.
12. Ibid.

SEVEN

SIN: THE ENEMY'S GREATEST THIEF

Even as I have seen, those who plow iniquity
and sow trouble reap the same.

—JOB 4:8

Amid all the positive teaching about success, inheritance, restoration, covenant, glory and destiny, why bring up sin? Very simply, because sin is the enemy's most effective and immediate weapon for robbing you of blessings and stopping God's purposes in your life and in the lives of the generations that follow you.

My prayer is that this chapter and the next will not only expose Satan's wiles and methods for keeping you in bondage to sin, but that these truths will also produce a great freedom that will thrust you forward into all that God has waiting for you.

SIN MOVES US OUT OF GOD'S PLAN

We have already talked a great deal about God's desire to bless us. He wants us to be successful, effective men and women of destiny in His kingdom. He longs for us to be fruitful and to continue to increase. He has an inheritance for us on this earth, just as He did for Adam. But we, like Adam, will find sin to be the factor that causes God blessings for us to come to a grinding halt. Sin has the power to smudge and even mutilate our lives. For now, let's consider four effects of sin.

1. Sin scatters. As mentioned in chapter 2, sin has a profound effect on our being as a whole. When we sin, pieces of the person God intends for us to be are left behind. We trade something God intended for us (a blessing, peace of mind, self-respect, intimacy with God or those we love, even physical health) for a sin we have committed. Parts of the blessed, whole, successful person God meant for us to be are, therefore, left scattered along the paths of our lives at every point where we have sinned and not turned back into a right relationship with God and those we've sinned against. Scattering is actually a curse that results because of sin.

Scattering has devastating effects. Here are some possibilities: Our relationships, both with God and others, may be difficult, or we may have experienced many broken relationships. Our paths may be unclear, and we seem to flounder, hoping for some direction. We are not firmly rooted in who we are in Christ and may be easily tossed around by new doctrines, or simply not able to stand for what we know is right. We may move around quite a bit looking for the perfect job, perfect spouse or perfect city that will finally make us happy. Scattering produces an unsettling, dissatisfied feeling. We know there must be more, but success always seems just out of our reach. Sin is often the root cause. We cannot walk into everything that God has for us to be until we have dealt with sin (both personal and generational) and allowed God to heal the fragmented, scattered parts of our lives.

One major cause of scattering is fornication and adultery. A biblical picture of what happens to us can be seen through Israel. The Bible says that when the Israelites played the harlot by seeking after other gods, God scattered them throughout the earth. When we have ungodly relationships, we literally scatter our seed where it does not belong, which results in scattered lives. We have formed ungodly soul ties with people other than our spouses. We may have produced illegitimate children. We have broken bonds of trust, if not with a spouse, then certainly with God. We have sinned against our own bodies. As a result, pieces of our lives and our affections are strewn here and there.

2. Sin steals our freedom. When I know that I am obeying God, I walk in freedom. When I know that I am in sin, I am in bondage. It's that simple. For instance, if I have filed an honest tax return, I don't think about it much past April 15th. If, however, I know I have cheated, I wait—sometimes years—to see if I will get caught. I wonder if I will get a letter from the IRS stating that they not only caught me, but now I owe the original taxes plus whatever penalties and interest they impose on the whole bill. I wonder if they will audit me and find other problems resulting in more taxes, penalties and interest. My cheating has put me in bondage, first to my own thoughts of getting caught, and then to the IRS for a lot more cash than I would have owed if I had only been honest.

With God and the spiritual realm, however, we don't have to wonder if we'll get caught—we already are. We cannot walk in the same freedom in our relationship with the Lord because there is something between us. *Any* sin we commit is first and foremost an offense against God, and until it is made right, we cannot expect to have an intimate relationship with Him. That is one way we are in bondage.

3. Sin moves us out from under our covenant protection. Another bondage that sin produces is an open door or "legal right" for Satan to steal what God has for us. When we choose to sin, we trade our spiritual protection over that part of our lives for the sin.

This is an aspect of the law of sowing and reaping. For instance, tithing is a biblical command. The first 10 percent of all our increase belongs to God whether we give it to Him or not. So if we choose not to obey God by giving Him what should already be His, we rob God. Based on the law of sowing and reaping, we are now subject to being robbed ourselves. That choice can now open us and our family to a spirit of poverty that may either keep us from having enough, or cause us to *fear* that we will not have enough.[1]

In either case, the spirit of poverty will cause us to rationalize that there is not enough or may not be enough for a full tenth of our income to be given away, much less anything over and above that. As the cycle continues, the spirit of poverty gains more and more control over how we handle our finances in general. Fear of poverty may not only keep us from tithing, but may even result in other forms of sin such as stealing, cheating, usury or compulsive gambling.

God's covenant plan for us may be to bring us great prosperity, but we have made the choice to move out from under His covenant protection in the area of finances by not obeying His command to give tithes and offerings. Until we get that part of our lives in order, we may also be dealing with a spirit of poverty that has depleted a part of our lives that God meant to overflow with blessing.

The same is true for any area of our lives in which we have sinned. We reap what we sow, and if we have sown outside of God's will for us, we will reap the same.

4. Sin builds a new belief system within us. When we sin, we begin to move away from the heart of God and from the principles He gave us for living our lives in blessing. As we move farther away, Satan has opportunities to affect our belief system so that those things which were once black and white are now varying shades of gray. We may come to believe that those little white lies aren't so bad, or that a little flirting with our spouse's friends is harmless. Our minds and our judgment become affected so we rationalize our behavior rather than confess it as sin to God.

THE AUTHOR OF SIN

Long before Adam and Eve ever considered crossing the will of God, Satan was adept at it. Satan was the first to ever sin, and He loves leading others in that direction. In his book *Warfare Prayer*, Dr. C. Peter Wagner defines Satan's motives this way:

> I think it is accurate to summarize all the evil and tactical activities of Satan in this statement: Satan's central task and desire is to prevent God from being glorified. Whenever God is not glorified in a person's life, in a church, in a city or in the world as a whole, Satan has to that degree accomplished his objective. The underlying motivation, as we are fully aware, is that Satan himself wants the glory due to God. As Lucifer fell from heaven, he was exclaiming, "I will be like the Most High!" (Isa. 14:14).[2]

♦

SATAN CANNOT TAKE OUR ETERNAL SALVATION FROM US, BUT HE CAN WORK TO ROB US OF OUR INHERITANCE AND DESTINY WHILE WE LIVE OUT OUR EARTHLY LIVES.

♦

As Wagner goes on to explain, Satan's primary objective is "to prevent God from being glorified by keeping lost people from being saved....Each time he succeeds he has won an *eternal victory*. Satan's secondary objective is to make human beings and human society as miserable as possible in the present life."[3] Whenever Satan can accomplish that task, he has won a *temporal victory*.

One of his main weapons for making us miserable is sin. Knowing all the consequences of sin, we can clearly see that sin is the easiest and most effective way to keep us bound and ineffective while on earth. Satan cannot take our eternal salvation from us, but he can work to rob us of our inheritance and destiny while we live out our earthly lives.

AGENTS OF DARKNESS

Satan himself is only a created being and, as such, cannot be in all places at all times. Therefore, he cannot fulfill his evil plans on earth without help. This is where demons come into play. They are agents of darkness sent to execute Satan's objectives in our lives. They have missed the goal of their primary objective for each person reading this book who has been saved. But their secondary objective, which is to make us as miserable as possible, will carry on throughout our times here on earth.

Do demons really affect our lives in the United States or Europe where we are sophisticated and scientifically enlightened? Dr. Charles Kraft of Fuller Theological Seminary says yes (here Kraft uses the word "demonization" to refer to demonic oppression or demonic attachment in an individual's life):

> (Church leaders) believe that our country has been so thoroughly influenced by Christianity that the Enemy couldn't be a serious threat here. Unlike many other Americans, these people believe in demons, but are deceived in several ways. First, they assume that the Christian influence in America has been sufficient to thwart demonization. Second, they assume that demonization will be obvious. Third, based on that assumption, they further assume that demonic activity occurs only where it is obvious, such as in other societies. They assume that Satan is intelligent enough not to use demonization here, but it doesn't occur to them that he is

clever enough to work evil in a less obvious manner than they have assumed is required.[4]

Later in his book *Defeating Dark Angels*, Kraft goes on to list activities that demonic forces carry out in the everyday lives of Christians and non-Christians alike:

1. We can assume that demons are involved in every kind of disruption....They push, prod, tempt, and entice to get people to make bad or at least unwise decisions.
2. Demons are probably the primary agents of temptation....Demons apparently can put thoughts in our minds, though, again, we are responsible for what we do with those thoughts. Since demons know what each of us is susceptible to, they will tailor the thoughts for the person. For example, demons seldom tempt a person in the sexual area who is not already vulnerable in that area.
3. Demons seek to keep people ignorant of their presence and activities....Demons like people to be ignorant of their presence and love it when people don't believe they exist.
4. Another demonic tactic is to get people to fear them. If they can't keep people ignorant, often their next strategy is to work on people's fears of what they don't understand.
5. In all satanic activity, deceit is a major weapon (which we will discuss later).
6. The job of demons is to hinder good by any possible means....They hinder unbelievers from believing (see 2 Cor. 4:4). They also work to undermine the faith of Christians. Worship, prayer, Bible study, expressions of love, and acts of compassion are high on the demonic hit list.
7. Demons, like Satan, are accusers. Dark angels regularly expose people to accusations of every kind....The self-rejection engendered by Western societies provides especially fertile ground for satanic accusation. They also like

to plant thoughts that lead us to accuse others, including God. Demons encourage rumors, cultivate misunderstandings, and justify anger at and blame of God.

8. Demons reinforce compulsions. Demons, of course, reinforce such compulsions as lust, drugs, alcohol....What is not so obvious is that they also encourage exaggerated attention to many things ordinarily considered "good." Among such compulsions are work, study, attractive dress, religion, doctrinal purity, family, achievement, and success.

9. Harassment: another demonic tool....I wager that they do whatever God allows to disrupt our lives through influencing such things as traffic, weather, health, stress, relationships, worship, sleep, diet, and machines (especially cars and computers).[5]

Each of these activities is meant to draw us in one way or other into sin and, in so doing, step out of God's plan for our lives. Each time we give in to these evil wiles, we have chosen not to glorify God and have opted instead to give the author of sin a temporal victory.

HOW PAM WAS FREED

My wife Pam and I went through a firsthand crash course in the different effects of demons and sin through something that happened many years ago in Pam's life.

PAM'S HISTORY

Pam was born into what some might have considered a perfect family. Her father was an aerospace engineer and her mother was a Texas beauty queen. Yet, many circumstances eventually gnawed away their ability to cope and both parents fell into alcoholism. As a result, Pam's early years were chaos.

The environment in their home finally got so bad that when she was 12 years old, Pam's father persuaded an aunt and uncle to legally adopt her out of the situation. The day after the adoption was finalized, her father committed suicide. Not only did she lose her father, but Pam never saw her natural mother again until attending her funeral in East Texas 20 years later. God did, however, have a redemptive plan for her life through the aunt and uncle who became as real parents to Pam, and her healing began.

A FRIEND DIES AND TROUBLE COMES ALIVE

One night, about five years after Pam and I were married, I was having difficulty falling asleep. I knew that something was wrong, so I stayed up until 2:00 A.M. praying. At 2:30 the phone rang, and it was someone from our church. The person called to tell us that the youth director's wife, Betsy, had been killed. Betsy was a pianist and had been playing for the Miss Texas Pageant that evening. On her way home, a drunk driver had hit her car and killed her. When I awakened Pam to tell her, she was understandably startled.

About three months later, Pam began having terrible problems. She had walked a narrow and committed path before the Lord ever since she was saved at the age of 12. She was also a very focused, stable individual. But Pam began struggling with her thoughts. During a course of months, she went from struggling over the reality of her salvation to thoughts of suicide. These thoughts were completely contrary to who Pam normally was.

We knew the source was demonic in nature, so we would read the Word and pray. But we could not gain victory because we could not find the root of it. Pam was just hanging on with everything she had.

AN ACT OF OBEDIENCE

One day, 16 grueling months later, I was scheduled to go to a friend's wedding vow-renewal service. I knew I was supposed to go; however, that day had been especially difficult for Pam. She was totally enveloped by a suicidal depression. But instead of getting upset, I asked the Lord what to do. It was as if He said, "I have told you where to go. You must obey Me when I direct your steps." So I got ready and left the house with Pam lying flat on the couch in a stupor.

When I got out on the sidewalk, I felt an evil presence accuse me, saying, "She will be dead when you return." Remembering what the Lord had said, I spoke back to the impression and said, "That is God's problem. I must obey God and do what He has asked me to do." So I went. When I got home, Pam was still lying there, battling with the demonic forces that were attacking her. But in some way, I knew I had won a victory over the enemy by obeying the Lord.

THE SECRET CONVERSATIONS OF HITLER

The next weekend our music director came to our home. Because we were planning a missions trip to the Native American reservation in New Mexico, we began discussing issues of spiritism and idolatry. He then asked me why people who have been involved in those things should burn the idols or fetishes. I explained that it was because the idolatry or spirit worship that was connected to those things needed to be purged from their lives. Burning those objects was a notice both to God and demonic forces that the person was no longer in bondage to the evil powers associated with those things, but was now totally reliant upon God and His power.

As we talked more about this, I told him that sometimes we burn things in obedience to God that may have spiritual significance we are unaware of. I then described an incident that had happened to me just two weeks prior. In my devotional time, I sensed the Lord telling me to sort through an old box of books from college and to burn the ones He showed me. I found several books in the box that I just threw out. But then I came across a book called *The Secret Conversations of Hitler*. I wondered where on earth that book had come from, but I knew I was to burn it. So I made a fire in the fireplace and tried to burn the book. At first, it would not burn. It seemed as though demonic forces had attached themselves to the book. Through much persistence, I finally forced the book to burn—it was bizarre!

As I recounted that story to the minister, Pam got a strange look on her face that made the hair on the back of my neck stand on end. When our friend left, I turned to Pam and asked where the book came from. She said that it had belonged to her natural father and was the only possession of his that she had left.

A VISITATION BRINGS FREEDOM

As we sat there, the Spirit of God began to descend upon us in a visitation. He began to give Pam an incredible revelation of the sinful and iniquitous pattern of unbelief that had been imbedded in her father and was now also in her. He showed her that on the night Betsy died, a demon had spoken to her mind and said, "There is no life after death."

Because Pam did not resist that thought and remained in passivity, those words took root in her heart and after a few months started creating unbelief in her. The deception opened the door for sin because she did not resist the devil with the Word of God to counteract his lie with the truth. She, therefore, had moved out of God's covenant protection for her. Pam immediately fell on her face weeping before the Lord and asking for forgiveness for sinning and allowing the deception to come into her inward parts. She renounced the false beliefs she had accepted in those months. That night God completely freed my beautiful wife from the demonic oppression she had been under. Since then, Pam has not struggled with unbelief over her salvation, nor with thoughts of suicide.

DECEPTION AND PRIDE

Satan uses two primary lures to trap us in sin: deception and pride. Because Satan is the father of all lies (see John 8:44), he and his demonic forces are particularly adept at deception. As Charles Kraft says, "He lies about who we are, he lies about who God is, he lies about who he is and what he does."[6] When we accept a lie, no matter how Satan got us to believe it, we transfer our belief from one Father (God) to believing another father (the enemy of our souls). That is what happened to Pam. She believed a lie about her salvation and life after death, and that lie was meant to kill her. But Pam took account-ability for her sin, and when she did, the deception broke so God could heal her. The truth, indeed, shall set you free (see John 8:36).

The two things that will hold us in deception are ignorance and pride. First, we must realize that God does not desire that we be ignorant. Our primary source of truth is the Word of God. You may be believing something about God, yourself or others that is contrary to the Bible. That is one reason we as Christians must know the Bible. The more we know what it really says, the less of an opening Satan has to lie to us. The belt of truth and the sword of the Spirit which is the Word of God (see Eph. 6:14,17) are, therefore, two very important elements of our spiritual armor as Christians.

AS MY GOOD FRIEND CINDY JACOBS OFTEN SAYS, "IF YOU DON'T THINK YOU CAN BE DECEIVED, YOU ALREADY ARE!"

Pride also works to hold us in deception. This happens when we refuse to acknowledge that we have been deceived because, after all, we know better. Pride is an especially vulnerable area for those who may have grown up in church or have pursued higher Christian education. Satan can be holding us in bondage to sin that we refuse to see. But as my good friend Cindy Jacobs often says, "If you don't think you can be deceived, you already are!"

UNBELIEF

A simple definition of unbelief is the feeling that God is not able to provide. If you have places in your mind and heart where you believe that God can't provide, you're in unbelief. Unbelief does not affect the character of God at all. God's faithfulness does not change because of our lack of faith. He remains the same. Unbelief just prevents God's blessings from permeating our lives, even when He desires to bless us. That's why when Jesus went into Nazareth, He couldn't do much (see Luke 4:16-30). Because of unbelief, the full will of God for that territory in that hour did not occur.

Unbelief can lead us into a process that overrides the promises of God. It can be triggered through ignorance, doubt, fear, rejection, bitterness, self-pity, self-exaltation, rationalism or false theology, to name a few. Regardless of what the Bible promises, unbelief counters it saying, "God cannot (or will not) intervene on my behalf. He cannot heal, deliver, provide or make a way. There is no miracle waiting for me."

Satan longs to set up a false belief system in our minds and hearts. As we allow our flesh to agree with those lies, the promises and inheritances God has for us become locked up so we can no longer access them.

REPROACHES

Sin produces what is known as a "reproach" and is defined as a source of blame, discredit, disgrace, shame, humiliation or scorn. Once sin is embedded in you, it creates a reproach that works against the favor of God. As we stated in chapter 4, favor means pleasure, desire, delight, to be pleased with or favorable toward something. When God is pleased with us, His favor rests upon us.

But sin can stop God's favor from resting upon us. In this case, we exchange God's favor for His disapproval. A reproach does not mean that we have lost our salvation or our standing with God. It does mean, however, that the favor God longs to give us in some areas of our lives is blocked because of the reproach. Until we make our lives right before God once again, we (and perhaps our descendants) will live under the effects of that reproach.

WHEN REPROACHES MANIFEST

Reproaches can be evidenced in a person's life in many ways. For example, let's look at two common manifestations:

1. An uncircumcised heart. In the Old Testament, the physical sign of the Abrahamic covenant was circumcision. When Joshua took the children of Israel into the Promised Land, all the circumcised males had died in the wilderness. Therefore, God told Joshua to renew the sign of circumcision throughout the new generation. *"So it was, when they had finished circumcising all the people, that they stayed in their places in the camp till they were healed. Then the Lord said to Joshua, 'This day I have rolled away the reproach of Egypt from you.' Therefore the name of the place is called Gilgal to this day"* (Josh. 5:8,9). This passage shows that by obedience to that command, God removed the last of the reproach from Egypt off the people. All the shame and disgrace of their slavery was gone.

Today, it is not a physical but a spiritual sign we bear, which is circumcision of the heart. Deuteronomy 30:6 explains: *"And the Lord your God will circumcise your heart and the heart of your descendants, to love the Lord your God with all your heart and with all your soul, that you may live."*

As we see in this verse, God will circumcise our hearts when we make the choice to love Him and to maintain our covenant with Him. A circumcised heart is one that is focused on the things of the spirit rather than the flesh. It is manifested in loving the Lord your God with all your heart and with all your soul, that you may live. Without circumcision of the heart, reproaches, such as slavery for the children of Israel, will not be fully broken off your life.

2. Illness. Reproaches caused by sin have much more of an effect on our basic bodily and mental functions than many of us realize. In fact, we know that *"the wages of sin is death"*—physical death (Rom. 6:23). By the same token, a result of sin is also illness. The most visible sin-initiated reproach on our society today is AIDS. While not every case of AIDS is a direct result of a specific sin, the majority are. In addition, certain forms of arthritis have been linked to anger. Ulcers and other stomach ailments can be caused by sin-induced anxiety. Even though not all illnesses are a result of sin (see John 9:3), many are and need to be addressed in that context.

OVERCOMING SIN

So, how do we move out of sin and back into our covenant place with God? The answer is through repentance. True repentance is undergoing transformation by the renewing of the mind. Romans 12:2 says, *"And do not be conformed to this world, but be transformed by the renewing of your mind, that you may prove what is that good and acceptable and perfect will of God."*

THE MIND AND THE HEART
"I will put My laws in their mind and write them on their hearts; and I will be their God, and they shall be My people" (Heb. 8:10).

First, we must establish the correlation between your mind and your heart. The word "mind" in the Bible is often synonymous with the word "heart." It is not uncommon to see two translations of the same verse in which one translates the word as "heart" and the other as "mind."

Being transformed by the renewing of your mind does not just mean your brain; it also means your heart. Here in Hebrews 8:10, we see how our minds and our hearts relate to our covenant with God. He puts His laws in our minds and writes them on our hearts. In other words, He establishes His boundaries within us. That's how covenant is formed. As we submit to those boundaries, God gives us the power to keep that covenant by being our God, as is promised in this passage. When we break that covenant through sin, His laws need to be reestablished within us—both in our minds and our hearts.

REPENTANCE THROUGH TRANSFORMATION
Repentance is, of course, at the very core of ridding sin from our lives. Many have been taught that to repent means to turn and go

in a different direction. That is true. But the first step is to change our minds about the matter. We must first decide the sin is not worth the price we pay, in our own lives and in the lives of future generations, as we will see in the next chapter. Then, once we've changed our minds and turned, we must allow our minds to be totally transformed and renewed by God.

As Francis Frangipane shows us, these steps of repentance through renewing our minds are crucial for gaining freedom from demonic forces that work to keep us in bondage to sin:

> Without some measure of repentance, deliverance is almost always impossible, for although a spirit may be commanded to leave, if the structure of the individual's thought has not been changed, his wrong attitude toward sin will welcome that spirit back....If you will truly walk with Jesus, many areas of your thinking processes will be exposed. There will be grace and a power from God to enable you to repent and believe God to impart His virtue into your life....You may be tempted to surrender just a token sin or some minor fault, while allowing your main problems to remain entrenched and well-hidden. The demon you are fighting is using your thoughts to protect his access to your life.[7]

Repentance and renewing our minds, therefore, is the only way to fight our fleshly natures and to ward off the onslaught of Satan and his demonic forces who seek at all costs to hold us in bondage. Let's take a look at the word "transformation" in order to understand the process we go through when allowing the Lord to renew our minds.

Trans means to cross over or go to the other side. Form means composition or structure. Transformation, therefore, means to cross over, or completely change composition or structure. When we allow God to transform us, we change our appearance to look more like Him. As we do that, we also change in potential. With a new structure, we also have new potential that begins to unlock in our lives.

A fierce battle is waging over our minds. God is longing to transform us so we can return to our place of covenant. The enemy is trying all forms of bondage to keep us from having an effective relationship with God. Thus, we can see that allowing our minds to be transformed by God does require warfare. We must learn, therefore, how to resist Satan in our minds and hearts. We have already discussed the importance of knowing and standing on Scripture. That is a key to not only resisting the devil, but also to allowing our minds to be transformed. As we cultivate deeper relationship with God, He will bring healing to our minds and hearts, but we must fight the battle of persistence in pursuing relationship with Him and shutting out the lies of Satan.

FORGIVENESS

Another crucial factor to moving out of sin is to walk in forgiveness. Jesus Himself taught us to pray, saying, *"And forgive us our sins, just as we have forgiven those who have sinned against us"* (Matt. 6:12, *NLT*). Immediately following these passages on how to pray, Jesus admonishes, *"If you forgive those who sin against you, your heavenly Father will forgive you. But if you refuse to forgive others, your Father will not forgive your sins"* (Matt. 6:14,15, *NLT*).

Forgiveness must have been a crucial point in the Lord's prayer for Jesus to have immediately decided to discuss this point rather than "give us this day our daily bread," or "Thy kingdom come, Thy will be done." Although Jesus certainly talks about these things at other times, the forgiveness issue was immediately reiterated. Why does God say that He will not forgive our sins if we will not forgive others? Again, it is the law of sowing and reaping.

As if God's forgiveness weren't enough, there are other ways we pay for unforgiveness. One is that it hinders our prayers from being heard by God. In Mark 11:24,25 Jesus says, *"Listen to me! You can pray for anything, and if you believe, you will have it. But when you are praying, first forgive anyone you are holding a grudge against, so that your Father in heaven will forgive your sins, too" (NLT).*

Unforgiveness also allows a bitter root to grow in our hearts. When we make the choice to refuse to forgive, a seed begins growing within us. That seed, watered by demonic forces that love to accuse, can take deep root within our hearts. The fruit of this growth is bitterness, which can lead to addictions, despondency, rage, hatred, resentment or controlling behaviors, to name just a few. We will never walk in the fullness of our inheritance while bitterness lives in our hearts.

Furthermore, if we do not forgive others, in a sense we bind ourselves to that person and to that event so that we cannot move forward in all that God intends for us. In his book *Spiritual Warfare for the Wounded*, Dr. Mark Johnson confirms this by saying,

> When we harbor unforgiveness we are—in essence—continuing to allow the person we won't or "can't" forgive, to control us. Until we forgive that person, we can't learn to live entirely in the present because we are not yet finished with the pain of the past. In forgiving our abusers, we take back the power that God intends for all humans to have—the power to choose to live wholly for Christ.[8]

Another perhaps even more sobering effect of unforgiveness is that it gives the enemy legal right into an area of our lives, which he holds in darkness. Demonic forces in our lives are often linked to unforgiveness. It is the food on which they feed. If we are unwilling to forgive, we constantly provide them with a diet that fuels their evil agendas. The more unforgiveness we give them, the stronger their influence grows in our lives.

Doris Wagner, a dear colleague of mine and an experienced practitioner in deliverance, will not even attempt delivering people from evil spirits until they come to a place of forgiveness toward anyone who has hurt them. She says it is a waste of time. Because if a person is unwilling to forgive, the demonic forces, even though they may be evicted for a short time, will always return. The unforgiveness has given them a legal right in that person's life. What's more, they often bring friends. When speaking of expelled demons who return to a person only to find their legal right to be there still intact, Matthew 12:45 says, *"Then he goes and takes with him seven other spirits more wicked than himself, and they enter and dwell there; and the last state of that man is worse than the first."* No wonder Doris will wait until the person is ready to forgive!

We have talked about several consequences of unforgiveness. Forgiveness, obviously, will produce the opposite effects in our lives. God can and will forgive us, and we can come under His covenant protection once again. Our prayers will be far more effective. We can become free from bitter roots. We free the other person from his or her debt to us, which propels us into our own future. We remove the legal right for certain demonic forces that are at work in our lives. Forgiveness produces freedom! And freedom is essential to possessing all the inheritance the Lord has for us.

Notes

1. For further study see Jack Hayford, *Glory on Your House* (Grand Rapids, Mich.: Chosen Books, 1982), pp. 184-201.
2. C. Peter Wagner, *Warfare Prayer* (Ventura, Calif.: Regal Books, 1992), p. 61.
3. Ibid.
4. Charles H. Kraft, *Defeating Dark Angels* (Ann Arbor, Mich.: Servant Publications, 1992), p. 44.
5. Ibid., pp. 102-110.
6. Ibid., p. 108.
7. Francis Frangipane, *The Three Battlegrounds* (Cedar Rapids, Iowa: Arrow Publications, 1989), p. 18.
8. Mark Johnson, *Spiritual Warfare for the Wounded* (Ann Arbor, Mich.: Servant Publications, 1992), p. 162.

EIGHT

UNDERSTANDING GENERATIONAL SIN AND INIQUITY

Blessed is the man who fears the Lord, who delights greatly in His commandments. His descendants will be mighty on earth; the generation of the upright will be blessed. Wealth and riches will be in his house, and his righteousness endures forever.

—PSALM 112:1-3

Not too many years ago I labored through a year fraught with illness. It seemed as though I was always battling something. As I do with every new year, I drew aside with the Lord to seek direction for the coming year. That particular day, I was bringing my health before Him, asking Him about the year ahead. The inner voice of the Holy Spirit seemed to say, "I don't want you to go around that mountain again. I will bring healing to you." That was fine with me because

I was sick of it—and I knew God was sick of it too. He wanted me to be free more than I did.

Shortly thereafter I was on a ministry trip when I sensed my blood pressure rising sky-high. As soon as I returned home, the doctor confirmed it. The prior year I would have said, "Oh, that's just life. It must be the price I am paying to preach the gospel." But in this new year I had just entered, I knew God had spoken and illness was not a part of His plan for me.

Later that night I went to a church service where the teaching focused on communion and on the hands of Christ. Feeling a divine nudge, I looked down at my own hands and saw an occult marking appear on my hand. A bit startled, I immediately asked the Lord what it was. As I did, I remembered a time from years prior when I had allowed my boss in the business world to read my palm. I had not thought about that incident in years! What's more, I remembered every word he said. I realized that I had violated a principle of God by using occult power. I also realized that I had never properly confessed the sin of that incident.

Then I recalled that my mother had also used occult power by going to a fortune-teller (which she renounced much later on). As my mind reflected further back, I recollected a scene with my grandfather. I was working with him one day when we encountered a wasps' nest in the middle of a doorway we were trying to enter. He just looked at his palm, spoke something to it, held it up, and every one of the wasps dropped dead right before our eyes. He had used occult power to kill them.

As I started remembering these kinds of incidents, I realized that the illness I had been suffering was actually a spirit of infirmity that had attached itself to me because of occultic involvement in my family's generations. Immediately I confessed it to God, asked forgiveness for me and my family, renounced it and took communion before the Lord.

Three days later I went back to the doctor. This time my blood pressure (which had routinely been running 140/100) was down to

100/70. I knew God had shown me the iniquity in my family so that I could make it right with Him, break the power of a spirit of infirmity, and allow Him to heal my body. That trip to the doctor's office was confirmation of His word to me and of His goodness in releasing me from the iniquitous pattern in my family of using occult power.

In each of our families God has a destiny to unlock, but Satan works to pervert that plan. He uses sin to embed a stream of weakness, known as iniquity, to control past, present and future generations and to keep them from God's divine plan. Let's look at how it works.

WHAT IS GENERATIONAL SIN AND INIQUITY?

"For I, the Lord your God, am a jealous God, visiting the iniquity of the fathers upon the children to the third and fourth generations of those who hate Me" (Exod. 20:5).

Difficult as it may be to understand in a society as individualistic as our own, the sins of our forefathers and foremothers can greatly affect who we are today, what spiritual challenges we face, and what sins we may be most susceptible to. Perhaps the easiest analogy we have for understanding how this occurs is through our knowledge of genetics. Just as we may inherit our mother's nose or our father's eyes, we may also inherit our mother's legalism or our father's alcoholism. Unrepentant sin can leave a spiritual weakness toward that sin in a family line (called iniquity) just as diabetes can leave a physical weakness toward diabetes in a family line.

The definition of sin is missing the mark or breaking the law of God. The definition of iniquity is a generational deviation from God's proper path. Because of *sin* in the generations, the *iniquity* of that sin can be passed on to the children. In her book *The Voice of God*, Cindy Jacobs defines the two this way:

> The Bible speaks of them as two different things. Sin is basically the cause, and iniquity includes the effect. Generational iniquity works like this: A parent can commit

a sin such as occultic involvement or sexual sin and that produces a curse. The curse then causes a generational iniquity or weakness to pass down in the family line.

Here is an example that might clarify this process. A pregnant woman is X-rayed and the unborn child becomes deformed by the X ray. The unborn child didn't order the X ray and is entirely a victim but, nonetheless, is affected by the X ray. Sin, like the X ray, damages the generations. This is an awesome thought and should put the fear of the Lord in us before we enter into sin.[1]

BIBLICAL EXAMPLES OF SIN AND INIQUITY

The Scriptures give a number of passages that allude to the concept of sin and iniquity in the generations. Here is some of what the Bible has to say:

He who speaks flattery to his friends, even the eyes of his children will fail (Job 17:5).

Prepare slaughter for his children because of the iniquity of their fathers, lest they rise up and possess the land, and fill the face of the world with cities (Isa. 14:21).

In those days they shall say no more: "The fathers have eaten sour grapes, and the children's teeth are set on edge" (Jer. 31:29).

[Speaking of the Lord] *You show lovingkindness to thousands, and repay the iniquity of the fathers into the bosom of their children after them* (Jer. 32:18).

Our fathers sinned and are no more, but we bear their iniquities (Lam. 5:7).

And all the people answered and said, "His blood be on us and on our children" (Matt. 27:25).

Therefore, just as through one man sin entered the world, and death through sin, and thus death spread to all men, because all sinned (Rom. 5:12,13).

In addition to these passages, there are several biblical stories that illustrate how generational sin and iniquity may have played out in the lives of key characters (I have derived these examples from various teachings by Cindy Jacobs).

KING DAVID

King David was an icon in Israel's history. He was a writer of numerous psalms, a great king in Israel, a mighty warrior, a worshiper who strengthened the worship of God throughout all of Israel, and a person described as a man after God's own heart (see Acts 13:22). Even so, as David reflects on his own life he says, *"Behold, I was brought forth in iniquity, and in sin my mother conceived me"* (Ps. 51:5).

In 1 Kings, David is described this way: "David did what was right in the eyes of the Lord, and had not turned aside from anything that He commanded him all the days of his life, except in the matter of Uriah the Hittite" (1 Kings 15:5).

The matter of Uriah the Hittite referred to here was David's downfall with Bathsheba (Uriah was her husband). How could such a man of God be so susceptible to blatant adultery? Perhaps it was the iniquity (spiritual weakness) of sin in David's lineage that could be traced back three generations. David, as it turns out, was a direct descendant of Rahab the harlot (see Matt. 1:5,6).

But the iniquity did not stop with David. We see that at least two of David's sons were affected by sexual sin. The constant influx of pagan wives and concubines into Solomon's court eventually led to his downfall as he began worshiping false gods. Amnon, another son of David, lusted after his own sister, Tamar, and eventually committed incest with her. The iniquity of sexual sin was an ongoing weakness in David's family line.[2]

Iniquitous patterns will also keep us from moving in God's timing. Notice that in this scenario with David and Bathsheba, the real issue was *"in the time when kings go to out to battle"* (2 Sam. 11:1). The sin pattern imbedded in David moved him out of God's timing and positioning, and kept him from his apostolic kingly function of warfare and protection over the nation. Iniquitous patterns always try to remove God's authority from you.

Because David was not in the right place at the right time, he opened himself up for the enemy's plan of demise. This caused him, if you will remember, to lose a portion of his inheritance. The child that was brought to birth by this illegal consummation died—an example of our seed not coming into its fullness because of iniquitous sin.

DEMONS WAIT UNTIL GOD HAS USED US GREATLY AND WE HAVE GATHERED MUCH INFLUENCE BEFORE EXPOSING THAT PLACE WHERE INIQUITY STILL HAS LEGAL ACCESS TO US. THEN THEY CAN ACT AS SATAN'S EMISSARIES OF TEMPTATION.

The enemy understands God's timing. Therefore, he knows how to ensnare us at the most opportune time to keep us from advancing the Kingdom. Matthew 8:29 says, *"What have we to do with You, Jesus, You Son of God? Have you come here to torment us before the time?"*

Demons know the iniquitous patterns within us, and at the time of our deliverance, they make a stand. They also wait until

God has used us greatly and we have gathered much influence before exposing that place where iniquity still has legal access to us. Then they can act as Satan's emissaries of temptation. That is why you see so many ministers reach a certain level of spiritual authority and then fall.

You may ask, "How in the world could this happen?" The answer is that Satan just bided his time, knowing that he still had access within that individual's life. Then at the right time with the right bait, he hooked in and not only pulled that person down, but everyone he or she was influencing. The result is not only an individual reproach, but also a corporate reproach that will have to be reconciled in God's process of time.

If David had stayed focused in God's purpose of his kingship, he would have overthrown the iniquitous pattern in his bloodline (Rahab/Salmon, Boaz/Ruth, Obed, Jesse, David). Notice David was the fourth generation of a bloodline that had an iniquitous pattern within it. Rahab was redeemed from the curse of Canaan by exercising faith in an intercessory-type act of hiding God's men when they came to find their entryway into the inheritance of Canaan. When all of Jericho was destroyed, Rahab was saved because of her act of obedience. She then entered into covenant with God's plan.

Any time we come into covenant with the plan of God, the iniquitous patterns within our ungodly inheritance weaken. Ruth, though a Moabite with an ungodly inheritance, so demonstrated covenant agreement with God's covenant plan and people that God used her to birth and propel His covenant plan for the future. Ruth birthed the lineage of the king—just because of covenant.

My study of the Scriptures has convinced me that if we remain in covenant, iniquity and sin can be annihilated by the third or fourth generation within a bloodline. We then form a godly inheritance that is transferred to the generations to come. However, Satan does not give up easily, and in any generation before a total annihilation of iniquity has occurred, he attempts to regain a foothold. Therefore, you may see a sin pattern lying dormant for three generations with a great leadership anointing like David had and that individual being used mightily in God's kingdom when Satan finds an inroad to a place that has not been crucified. Just at the time of total annihilation, the entire iniquitous pattern is brought to rebirth and the whole cycle of sin and death is repeated, usually in a multiplied manner. This is what we find with Solomon. Therefore, any generation can reinforce a demonic stronghold or pattern, and instead of annihilating the curse, instead strengthen it for the generations to come.

What I believe is this: Iniquitous patterns can actually overtake a bloodline and form a godless group of people on earth, forcing God to remove the iniquitous pattern through judgment. This is why entire people groups are wiped out.

NOAH

Another biblical example of sin and iniquity is Noah and his son Ham. In Genesis 6:9 we read, *"This is the genealogy of Noah. Noah was a just man, perfect in his generations. Noah walked with God."* At this point in the story we can infer that Noah was living without any iniquity in his life.

After the flood, however, grave sin did enter the family lines through Noah's son Ham in a drunken incident. Genesis 9:21,22 tells us, "Then he [Noah] drank of the wine and was drunk, and became uncovered in his tent. And Ham, the father of Canaan, saw the nakedness of his father, and told his two brothers outside."

Some commentaries argue that to "uncover" can mean anything from looking upon lustfully to sexual relations. The term, however, is not benign or innocent. It is always used with sexual connotations, even in Levitical law, which says, "None of you shall approach anyone who is near of kin to him, to uncover his nakedness: I am the Lord" (Lev. 18:6). The *International Standard Bible Encyclopedia* further tells us that the term "nakedness" was almost certainly used in this passage as a euphemism for a particularly horrible act.[3]

My theory about Noah is that Ham's sin was not just a sexual issue. Ham actually took advantage at a weak point in Noah's fatherhood to attempt to steal his authority. We find that Shem and Japheth took a garment and laid it on both of their shoulders and went backward and covered the nakedness of their father. Evidently, in Ham's defiling sin, he took his father's garment illegally. (Absalom attempted to do the same thing with David. Jezebel tried to do the same thing in Israel.)

Whether Ham committed a sexual act with his father, or just lusted after him, we will never know. We do know, however, that whatever sin Ham committed, that day changed the life of his son Canaan and the face of generations to follow. Noah was so angry about what happened that he cursed Ham's son: "So Noah awoke from his wine, and knew what his younger son had done to him. Then he said: 'Cursed be Canaan; a servant of servants He shall be to his brethren'" (Gen. 9:24,25).

That incident of sin brought great iniquity into the family line. Noah, instead of blessing his children and children's children, released a curse on Ham's younger son, Canaan. This curse dictated that instead of being a leader, Canaan would have to be a servant from that day forward, which is why I think it was a leadership issue. This child could easily have been destined to be a leader in God's army, but because of the sins of the father, that redemptive gift was robbed. The curse on Canaan actually affected an entire territory. And notice what it removed: God's inheritance that He had promised to Abraham. The curse that was perpetuated from generation to generation actually overtook the boundaries of land that had been promised in God's original covenant. Talk about usurping!

Canaan eventually fathered 11 nations whose peoples settled along the Mediterranean sea coast, then moved inland and eventually founded the cities of Sodom and Gomorrah. As we know, these cities and their inhabitants were later destroyed by God for immorality, including rampant homosexuality as we see when the men of the city demanded that Lot send out his male visitors so they could have sex with them (see Gen. 19:5).

The sin was, therefore, the homosexual intent or activity of Ham toward Noah. The iniquity was blatant homosexuality and ungodliness that grew throughout the generations to the point that God was forced to destroy whole cities (Sodom and Gomorrah).[4] Following the same thought, the sin was Ham usurping his father. The iniquity actually spread throughout all of the "ites" and controlled an entire territory, usurping God's covenant plan throughout that region.

As we see in the case of Sodom and Gomorrah, entire cities and territories can be affected by generational sin. A territorial iniquity can affect people living in an area or belonging to a particular people group. Four specific kinds of sin make a territory or a people group particularly susceptible to territorial iniquity: (1) forms of idolatry; (2) bloodshed; (3) occult activity; and (4) immorality patterns permeating the society.

Remember that in the covenant God established with Abraham in Genesis 15, the Lord set the boundaries for the inheritance of His people. Those boundaries included all the sin that had multiplied through the "Curse of Canaan." The Lord told Abraham that He would give his generations the ability to receive all the blessings within those boundaries. However, He stipulated that they would have to wait until the iniquity of the Amorites was complete.

The Lord did not want a generation to prematurely go to war until they could gain all the spoils that this iniquitous pattern had been amassing. Thus, the whole issue of staying in God's time is that within the process of time, God will transfer the wealth that the enemies in your line have amassed. In this case, He said the fourth generation would go in and gain all the wealth that the Amorites had been amassing in God's inheritance and covenant boundaries. Now notice that the fourth generation set out to do this but was stopped along the way. Therefore, only those in the fourth generation who maintained the faith of God's covenant, Joshua and Caleb, were able to go in for the transference of wealth from Canaan.

Actually the fifth generation began to receive the overall benefits. But remember, and I will come to it in a moment, this group did not fully obey God's plan to wipe out the iniquitous patterns of the territory. So these iniquitous patterns continued to influence them throughout history.

A NINETEENTH-CENTURY STUDY

We have looked at a few biblical examples of generational sin and iniquity. Now we will look at how this concept plays out in more modern times. In Noel and Phyl Gibson's book *Evicting Demonic Intruders*, they give this fascinating sociological study to help support the idea of generational sin (and blessings!) being passed down family lines:

Around the beginning of the twentieth century, a Mr. E. E. Winship published studies of two well-known American families of the nineteenth century. His findings have been featured in many publications since that date and are well worth passing on:

Max Jukes was an atheist who married a godless woman. Some 560 descendants were traced. Of these:

- 310 died as paupers.
- 150 became criminals, 7 of them murderers.
- 100 were known to be drunkards.
- More than half the women were prostitutes.

In all, the descendants cost the U.S. government one and a quarter million 19th-century dollars.

Jonathan Edwards was a contemporary of Max Jukes. He was a committed Christian who married a godly young lady. Some 1,394 descendants were traced. Of these:

- 295 graduated from college, from whom 13 became college presidents and 65 became professors.

- 3 were elected as United States senators, 3 as state governors, and others sent as ministers to foreign countries.
- 30 were judges.
- 100 were lawyers, one the dean of an outstanding law school.
- 56 practiced as physicians, one was dean of a medical school.
- 75 became officers in the army and navy.
- 100 were well-known missionaries, preachers, and prominent authors.
- Another 80 held some form of public office, of whom 3 were mayors of large cities.
- One was the comptroller of the U.S. Treasury, another a vice-president of the United States.

Not one of the descendants of the Edwards family was a liability to the government.[5]

HOW GENERATIONAL SIN AFFECTS US

Sins that are passed down through the generations have a strong influence on who we may become. Let's take a look at how generational sin can directly affect us.

INIQUITOUS PATTERNS

Have you ever noticed how things such as alcoholism, divorce, laziness or greed tend to run in families? These aren't just learned behaviors. They are manifestations of iniquity that have been passed down through the generations, or are iniquitous patterns. Of course there are isolated instances of sin that seem to have nothing to do with previous generations. In those cases, however, a new iniquitous pattern may be beginning in a family if that sin is not made right before God. But if you start looking around you with this in mind, you may be surprised at how many iniquitous patterns of sin you can find in family lines.

Having iniquity in a family line does not necessarily mean that every child will inherit that iniquity. Again, it's like inheriting a particular nose; some children will and some children won't. We can also see iniquity skip a generation. A three-generation family may look like this: The grandfather may be a compulsive gambler, never quite able to bring home his full paycheck without spending some or all of it on the horses. The father, on the other hand, may be a hardworking, honest man who always provides for his family and never even considers gambling as an option. Yet his college-aged son is having trouble saving for a car because he can't resist buying a fistful of lottery tickets or joining the Saturday night poker game.

The Jebusites are another example of iniquity not being annihilated in the third or fourth generation. Joshua and the people of Israel were commanded by God to annihilate all the "ites" as they took their portion of the inheritance He had allotted through the covenant of Abraham. The Bible says in Joshua 15:63, *"As for the Jebusites, the inhabitants of Jerusalem, the children of Judah could not drive them out; but the Jebusites dwell with the children of Judah at Jerusalem to this day."* (One interesting study I have done that gives me insight on how to pray for Israel today is how the "ites" are still in the land.) This iniquitous stronghold from the curse of Canaan was not overthrown until four generations later by David. So actually this generational iniquity stayed in place for eight generations.

Before David received his full kingship, he was required by God in 2 Samuel 5 to overthrow this people and the iniquitous pattern that had multiplied since the time of Ham's son. "Nevertheless David took the stronghold of Zion" (v. 7). God never forgets an iniquitous pattern. He will either find a generation that will overthrow that stronghold, or he will overthrow it Himself. I believe David's obedience in overthrowing this stronghold released the ark of God's presence back to its place in Jerusalem.

We have another case of a sin creating an iniquitous pattern that extended to the tenth generation. In Deuteronomy 23:2,3, we see issues of illegitimate birth and being a bastard. A consequence of this sin and iniquitous pattern kept any of that person's descendants from entering the assembly of God. This is where we see the grace of the new covenant. Jesus Christ came to fulfill the law and the prophets. The redemptive plan for humankind exhibited on the Cross at Calvary broke the power of illegitimate seed and being a bastard child and released the spirit of adoption. So any of us in any generation can be adopted and appropriate the power of God's rich inheritance and spiritual blessing in our bloodlines. Where our bloodlines without redemption were destined for an eternal damnation in hell, we now have access to the blood of the King that can redeem us fully.

FAMILIAL SPIRITS

Through sin and an iniquitous pattern, a familial spirit controls a certain person in a family. As we discussed in the last chapter, Satan and his demonic cohorts are hard at work trying to cause us as much misery as possible through sin. Sin is an opening for demonic forces to work in subsequent generations of a family through the iniquity produced. Familial spirits know the family weaknesses and, therefore, tempt family members with those weaknesses into the same or related sins. Some have been in families for generations on end.

Familial spirits, however, seldom work alone. Other spirits may also be involved. Again, using gambling as an analogy: Suppose there is also an older daughter in the family who is on her own. The daughter, no matter how hard she works, keeps going further into debt because she can't pay her bills. She may be living under a spirit of poverty.

How does that tie in with gambling? In the natural, it is easy to see how compulsive gambling can produce poverty. In the spiritual realm, a spirit of gambling will very often team up with a spirit of poverty, bringing the whole family into financial bondage, all because of one person's sin. The daughter may or may not have ever gambled, but because of the iniquity in her family line, she is suffering the consequences by living under a spirit of poverty.

Familiar spirits should not be confused with *familial* spirits. Familial spirits operate within family bloodlines. Familiar spirits are not confined in that way. They operate within the context of relationships that are formed when two people commit a similar or related sin. A familiar spirit causes the two to come into an agreement of sin. At the time of this writing, much of the headline news has been about a series of school shootings. One in Jonesboro, Arkansas, involved two young boys who plotted to carry out the fatal attack. A familiar spirit may well have been at work between the two boys as they came into agreement to commit such a horrible act.

FAMILY CURSES

Following the sudden death of Michael Kennedy, the cover of *Newsweek* magazine read, "The Kennedy Curse." In describing the reaction to Kennedy's death, the magazine reports, "Most Americans, hearing the news that Bobby's star-crossed son Michael had died in a skiing accident on New Year's Eve, may have felt that there is a curse on the House of Kennedy. The TV images eerily evoked so many earlier Kennedy family tragedies."[6]

The article goes on to expound on the younger Kennedy's life and, interestingly enough, makes this connection: "He always had to deal with the Kennedy name. The pressure was apparently too much. Michael began to exhibit other, less admirable Kennedy traits, like lust for forbidden sex and addiction to alcohol."[7] The author of this article may or may not have spiritual understanding of such things, but he did hit on a spiritual truth: Generational sin produces family curses.

The dictionary definition of a curse is the cause of evil, misfortune or trouble. John Eckhardt of Crusaders Ministries defines it as follows:

A curse is God's recompense in the life of a person and his or her descendants as a result of iniquity. The curse causes sorrow of heart and gives demonic spirits legal entry into a family whereby they can carry out and perpetuate their wicked devices.[8]

Eckhardt goes on to quote Derek Prince's seven common indications of a curse, which are chronic financial problems, chronic sickness and disease, female problems (I would add barrenness, whether brought on by the husband or the wife), accident proneness, marital problems, premature death and mental illness. Eckhardt adds mistreatment and abuse by others and wandering or vagabond tendencies to the list.[9]

Such curses are produced because of the law of sowing and reaping (see Job 4:8). When sin takes hold in the generations, a family curse is part of the effects of that sin. A curse is the opposite of blessing. When Adam and Eve sinned, they went from a state of being blessed to being cursed. When they sinned, they moved out from under their covenant blessing with God. In that case, God pronounced the curse over them. That curse has and will affect every single subsequent generation to live on this earth.

ANY TIME WE CHOOSE TO MOVE OUT FROM UNDER THE BLESSINGS OF GOD THROUGH SIN, WE ARE SUBJECT TO A CURSE.

Any time we choose to move out from under the blessings of God through sin, we are subject to a curse. There is not a "sinner's no-man's-land" where, if you only go this far with a sin, you may not necessarily be blessed but not necessarily be cursed either. The reason is because when we sin, we move out from under the shadow of God's covenant wing of protection. And as we do, Satan has more access to our lives. He won't pass up any chances we give him. He is as a roaring lion seeking to kill and destroy (see 1 Pet. 5:8), and when he has access to us, he will work to do just that.

Chronic problems such as those previously mentioned will continue to plague a family's bloodline until either the iniquity has played out (which means going three to four generations without repeating the initiating sin, despite the weakness toward it. If at any point, however, a family member falls back into the same sin, the iniquity begins again), or until the curse is broken through the power of the Cross.

Charles Kraft, who is very experienced in the field of deliverance, writes, "We once worked with a woman whose ancestry included seven generations of handicapped women. After the curse was broken and the woman was freed of the demon, she gave birth to a healthy baby girl."[10] I have already explained how iniquitous patterns can go from one generation to another. Here is a case of breaking that pattern in the seventh generation and restoring God's pattern of wholeness.

SPIRITUAL STRONGHOLDS

Another effect of generational iniquities are spiritual strongholds. Ed Silvoso, president of Harvest Evangelism, provides what is perhaps the best definition of a stronghold:

> A spiritual stronghold is a mind-set impregnated with hope-lessness that leads us to accept as unchangeable situations that we know are contrary to the will of God....Strongholds are built in the believer's mind by Satan so he can manipulate behavior without being detected.[11]

Silvoso's definition comes from 2 Corinthians 10:4,5, which says, *"For the weapons of our warfare are not carnal but mighty in God for pulling down strongholds, casting down arguments and every high thing that exalts itself against the knowledge of God, bringing every thought into captivity to the obedience of Christ."*

These are places in our minds that say, "Not even God can change this circumstance in my life," or, "There is no hope." In the last chapter I told the story of how my wife Pam struggled with suicidal thoughts because of unbelief. The demonic forces who were trying to destroy her were using a stronghold that caused her to take a drastic spiral.

In his book *The Three Battlegrounds*, Francis Frangipane helps us begin to discover what strongholds may be affecting us:

> If you want to identify the hidden strongholds in your life, you need only survey the attitudes in your heart. Every area in your thinking that glistens with hope in God is an area which is being liberated by Christ. But any system of thinking that does not have hope, which feels hopeless, is a stronghold which must be pulled down.[12]

Strongholds are produced by accepting a lie. It doesn't matter how cunning the devil was in presenting it—once we *accept* a lie, we fall into sin that will produce a stronghold. Strongholds can affect whole families through means such as superstition, mocking God, mocking biblical truth, unbelief, idolatry, legalism or atheism, to name a few. These thought processes can become so entrenched in the minds of family members that, until those strongholds are torn down, it becomes impossible, even as Christians, to walk into the destiny God has for them.

THE DNA FACTOR

We have discussed some of the spiritual reasons for our susceptibility to generational sin and iniquity, but there may be another factor involved: our DNA. Could the tendency toward committing the same sins as our mothers or grandfathers actually have become encoded in our genes?

Consider this: Adam and Eve were both created to live eternally upon this earth (see Gen. 2:17). They were never meant to die. Apparently God encoded that fact into their DNA. However, since the wages of sin is death, when Adam and Eve sinned, something in their physical bodies changed. They now had a biological clock that ticked down the time toward death. Because of sin, it is possible that something in their DNA—the blueprint that tells the body what to do—changed from producing endless life to an aging process that ultimately produced death. If so, corruptible DNA has passed on to their children and to every generation since.

Is it also possible that predisposition to certain types of sin actually become encoded in a family's DNA? *Life* magazine recently ran a cover feature entitled "Were You Born That Way?" In the article they suggest that there is a potential for such a link. When exploring addictive disorders the article states:

> "I started smoking at fifteen, mostly to be cool," says musician Kid Congo Powers, 37, who smokes four packs a day and is a recovering heroin addict and alcoholic. Powers comes from a long line of smokers and drinkers; twin studies bear out a genetic influence on addiction. Alcohol, heroin and tobacco elevate levels of dopamine, the brain chemical linked to euphoria. Researchers have found that some alcoholics and heroin addicts have an unusually long version of a gene on chromosome 11—the same gene that is common in risk-takers. This may not be surprising, given studies showing that risk-takers are more likely than others to start smoking, drinking or using drugs in the first place.[13]

One method scientists are using to determine the effect our DNA plays in our behavior is the "twin studies," in which they study identical twins who have grown up in different environments to check for behavioral similarities. The *Life* article goes on to tell of this amazing twin study:

> Identical twins separated five weeks after birth (Jim Lewis and Jim Springer) were raised by families 80 miles apart in Ohio. Reunited 39 years later, they would have strained the credulity of the editors of *Ripley's Believe It or Not*. Not only did both have dark hair, stand six feet tall and weigh 180 pounds, but they spoke with the same inflections, moved with the same gait and made the same gestures. Both loved stock car racing and hated baseball. Both married women named Linda, divorced them and married women named Betty. Both drove Chevrolets, drank Miller Lite, chain-smoked Salems and vacationed on the same half-mile stretch of Florida beach. Both had elevated blood pressure, severe migraines and had undergone vasectomies. Both bit their nails. Their heart rates, brain waves and IQs were nearly identical. Their scores on personality tests were as close as if one person had taken the same test twice.[14]

Although this is an extraordinary case, it does seem to suggest that certain predispositions are inherited in the family line. Could it be that generational sin, therefore, actually affects the very DNA we inherit? Could sin actually corrupt our physical makeup in addition to our spiritual makeup? Do we then pass that on to our children along with the color of their eyes? This could be one explanation for why iniquity does not affect every child in the same way. It may also explain why iniquity, like the tendency to bear twins, sometimes skips a generation.

An article published by the secular magazine *Men's Health* claims that "if someone in your family tried to commit suicide, you may be six times as likely to try it yourself."[15] The writer backs up that statement with the following study:

A Danish study followed 114 adopted boys—57 with a biological-family history of suicide, and 57 without. All the boys were raised by families with no history of suicide. Amazingly, the boys who later committed suicide had six times more biological relatives who had killed themselves than the boys who didn't commit suicide, "which should tell us that some people do seem genetically inclined that way." says Dr. Mann.[16]

One photo caption accompanying the article reads "Father and son: Shane DuBow still has warm memories of his dad, but he wonders what demons he may have inherited."[17] The writer of this article may have only been reaching for literary drama with that caption, yet he found himself much closer to the truth than he may have realized.

Does this give us a right to use our DNA as an excuse to sin? Paul answers this very clearly in Romans 6. God forbid, no! When the absolute truth of the covenant comes into our belief systems or cognitive processes, we are forced to make a choice. Therefore, it does not matter what goes on in your bloodline from generation to generation to generation, the truth can set you free.

As you embrace that truth and it goes down into your inner being, the truth actually changes your gene DNA structure. The Bible talks about this in Hebrews 4:12: *"For the word of God is...sharper than any two-edged sword, piercing even to the division of soul and spirit, and of joints and marrow, and is a discerner of the thoughts and intents of the heart."* Life is in the blood, and the blood is produced from the marrow. Once we embrace the Word of God and its covenant life-giving power, the DNA factor of our blood is actually transformed by the Spirit of God. Our conscience is cleansed, and we begin to operate in a new inheritance. Thank God for the Spirit of Adoption.

Whether or not it is passed on through our DNA, generational sin and iniquity is a fact of life. It was passed down to us and we will pass it on to our children, unless we understand and know God's remedy for the situation. Now that we know what generational sin and iniquity are, let's look at how we can overcome the problem.

HOW TO DETECT FAMILY INIQUITY

To detect the sins and iniquities that afflict your family, you will need to search for the patterns of sin that have been in your family lines. For example, look for statements about your family members such as, "George has a temper just like his grandfather," or "Sally really likes her wine, but then, so did Mom."

As you think through some possibilities, consider the following list of possible generational sins. While I have added to it, the basis for this list comes from Australian deliverance experts Noel and Phyl Gibson.

- Addictions of all kinds including drugs, alcohol, nicotine, gambling, food, compulsive physical exercise, compulsive spending, wild parties, etc.
- Mental problems including anxiety, worry, depression, schizophrenia, suicide, uncontrollable anger or rage, etc.
- Sexual problems including incest, homosexuality, frigidity, fornication, adultery, compulsive masturbation, prostitution, pedophilic behavior, pornography, bestiality, etc.
- False and deceptive religious tendencies including atheism, false cults, doctrinal heresies, religious bigotry, secret societies, etc.
- God-hating problems including mockery, hard-heartedness, sneering at God, unbelief, anti-Semitism, desecration, lawlessness, etc.
- Issues of the heart including bitterness, coveting, rebellion, greed, hatred, jealousy, judgmentalism, legalism, lust, being puffed up, laziness, resentfulness, stubbornness, being unforgiving, unloving, without pity, etc.
- Issues of sin toward others including betrayal, broken

promises, abortion, argumentativeness, fighting, gossiping, kidnapping, lying, manipulation or control, murder, prejudice, strife, thievery, cursing, disobedience, etc.
- Occultism and witchcraft practices including occultic visions, astrology, clairvoyance, psychic sensitivity or control, mind or thought control, ouija board, palm reading, psychic healing, seances, spiritism, sorcery, superstition, tarot cards, voodoo, witchcraft, yoga, fortune telling, etc.[18]

This is by no means an exhaustive list, but it might help as you think about the issues that have been present in your family line.

Once you have identified some sin patterns, think of what problems afflict your family. Is there poverty, divorce, rebellion in children? Have there been untimely deaths, accidents or chronic illnesses? These could all be the results of curses or familial spirits at work. Ask the Lord to identify the root sin issue that is behind the problem.

GOD'S REMEDY FOR INIQUITY

Hebrews 9:22 spells out God's remedy for sin: *"Without the shedding of blood, there is no forgiveness"* (*NIV*). In fact, the only remedy for sin and iniquity is the shedding of blood. There is no other way.

Joshua 7:1-26 tells us that Achan and his entire family were put to death because Achan took forbidden loot from Jericho. Because the blood of Achan's family was shed, the entire nation of Israel was cleansed from Achan's sin. In another instance recorded in 2 Samuel 21, seven of Saul's descendants were killed because Saul had broken a covenant agreement with the Gibeonites. By spilling the blood of Saul's decendants, a famine was broken off the land.

You might say, "But these were the Gibeonites—they were a part of the curse of Canaan. Why did God judge all of Israel for what Saul did to them?" The answer is that the Gibeonites, as you may recall, came into the agreement of God when they formed a covenant with Joshua. They never violated that covenant from that time forth. Also, they became servants to the Israelites as part of the covenant Joshua made with them. If you remember, that was within the boundaries of what Noah spoke to Ham—that Canaan's descendants would "serve." Therefore, they were in obedience to God's plan for them, and they had become servants to the covenant of God. God judged Israel because Saul violated God's covenant and plan for a people group by killing the Gibeonites.

Blood is the sacrifice that God requires to purify us from sin. Praise God that the blood of Christ is sufficient to cleanse us from all unrighteousness, including generational sin and iniquity. Speaking prophetically of Jesus, Isaiah 53:11,12 says, *"He shall see the labor of His soul, and be satisfied. By His knowledge My righteous Servant shall justify many, **for He shall bear their iniquities.** Therefore I will divide Him a portion with the great, and He shall divide the spoil with the strong, because He poured out His soul unto death, and He was numbered with the transgressors, and He bore the sin of many, and made intercession for the transgressors"* (emphasis added).

THE EXCHANGE OF BLOOD

When we came into relationship with God through Christ, we actually entered into a blood covenant with Him (see Matt. 26:28 and parallels: Mark 14:24; Luke 22:20; 1 Cor. 11:25). In that moment a divine exchange took place. God released the holy blood of Christ to make atonement for our sins.

Enormous power is available to us in the blood of Christ beyond our initial salvation. We, however, must choose to appropriate that power just as we did when we first came to Christ—salvation was available to us, but we were not actually saved until we came to God and accepted Christ. Through the power of Christ's blood, we can exchange such things as curses for blessings; guilt for purity; sickness for health; lack for provision; sorrow for joy; slavery for freedom and death for eternal life.

There is also another exchange that the blood of Christ can accomplish for us. As we ask the Lord, He will release the blood of Christ to atone for generational sin and supersede our *bloodline* to bring us back into His full plan for us. We then have the spiritual authority to break generational curses, cast out familial spirits and tear down strongholds. What a great deal! Now let's look at the steps for breaking generational iniquities.

BREAKING THE POWER OF GENERATIONAL SIN AND INIQUITY

The very first step in breaking the power of generational sin and iniquity is to repent for our own sin. No matter how much of a tendency you or I inherited in our family lines, that tendency is no excuse for the sin we have chosen to commit. We must be sure that we have clean hands and a pure heart before God (see Ps. 24:4), which is more than just saying, "Forgive me for all my sin. Amen." It means taking a hard self-inventory and repenting to God for each specific unrepentant sin in your life.

The second step, which we have already discussed, is to identify the generational sins that are at work in your family.

The third step is to be sure that you have forgiven your ancestors for bringing sin into the family line. John 20:23 says, *"If you forgive the sins of any, they are forgiven them; if you retain the sins of any, they are retained."* This verse serves to affirm the fact that power of that sin will not be broken if we carry unforgiveness in our hearts. Any unforgiveness is enough for demonic forces to maintain their power in any given area. Go to the Lord, therefore, and be sure you have no bitterness or anger in your heart toward those who initiated or perpetuated bondage in your family.

The fourth step is repenting for the sin in your generations. We do have the authority to ask God to forgive someone in our generational line for their sin. That does not mean that whoever first committed the sin will not have to stand before God and make an accounting for it. Each individual is responsible to God for his or her own actions as is established in Ezekiel 18. It does mean, however, that we can appropriate the blood of Christ into our bloodline where that sin has been committed, and break the power of that sin in the generations. We must then renounce that sin in the family line. By so doing, we remove Satan's legal right to continue tormenting ourselves and our children in that area.

The following is a sample prayer for repenting of sin in the generations:

> Father, in the name of Jesus, on behalf of my family (be specific, if you know who sinned) I repent for the sin of (again, be as specific as you can) to the third and fourth generation back. Lord, I declare that when I am tested, the Spirit of God will arise within me for You have given me the power to become a child of God. I thank You that the iniquitous patterns in my bloodline will not be reproduced or reinforced, but will be annihilated. I thank You for the blood of Jesus, and I appropriate its power in my family line. By the power and authority of that blood, I now renounce that sin in the family line. I thank You, Lord, that You say when we are weak, You are strong. I ask that You bring strength into that area of weakness in me and my family.
>
> Now, in the name of Jesus, I come against the iniquity of _____, and I break its power over me and over my children and over my children's children. Satan, you no longer have authority to torment me or my children with this iniquity, for God promises in Hebrews 8:12 that He will be merciful to our unrighteousness, and that these sins and lawless deeds He will remember no more! In Jesus' name, I pray. Amen!

WHEN MORE WARFARE IS NEEDED

When a generational sin has already become entrenched in you or your children before you knew how to pray this way, an extra measure of warfare may be needed to see the power of that sin broken. Remember, if you are praying for your children, they still have a free will and must make their own choices. But the following are some ways that might help clear out spiritual "clutter" so they can choose without the help of demonic forces assigned to blind them.

1. Fast. Fasting is a powerful weapon we have in our arsenal against the enemy. Isaiah 58 gives us some insight as to how fasting helps us wage warfare:

> *Is this not the fast that I have chosen:* **To loose the bonds of wickedness, to undo the heavy burdens, to let the oppressed go free, and that you break every yoke?** *Is it not to share your bread with the hungry, and that you bring to your house the poor who are cast out; when you see the naked, that you cover him, and not hide yourself from your own flesh? Then your light shall break forth like the morning,* **your healing shall spring forth speedily, and your righteousness shall go before you; the glory of the Lord shall be your rear guard** (vv. 6-8, emphasis added).

As you fast, ask the Lord to loose the bonds of wickedness, to undo heavy burdens, to let the oppressed go free and to break the yoke of that sin over yourself or your child.

2. Pray God's Word. Just as we did in the last paragraph, we can begin to see that praying Scripture is a powerful spiritual weapon! God's Word is alive and full of great promises and truths that dispel the enemy's lies in our lives. Ask God for a promise from His Word; then use it. Repeat it both to God (this strengthens your faith) and to Satan (who hates the truth of the Word of God) as often as is necessary.

Here is an example of how to pray Scripture:

> God, this situation looks like an immovable rock in my life, but your Word declares, *"Is not My work like fire [that consumes all that cannot endure the test]? says the Lord, and like a hammer*

that breaks in pieces the rock [of most stubborn resistance]?" (Jer. 23:29, *Amp.*, emphasis added).

Thank you, Lord, that Your work is a hammer that is powerful enough to break this stubborn, resistant rock into pieces.

3. Do not be weary in battle. God will complete the work He has begun!! Ephesians 3:20 says, *"Now to Him **who is able** to do exceedingly abundantly above all that we ask or think, **according to the power that works in us**, to Him be glory in the church by Christ Jesus to all generations, forever and ever. Amen"* (emphasis added). Remember that it is His power that is doing the work. Weariness comes from thinking we have to make it happen. And the result of weariness is discouragement.

Discouragement causes us to give up, even when we have the keys for victory! Understanding generational sin and iniquity is one of the major keys to possessing your inheritance. Allow the Lord to bring times of refreshing into your life as He leads you on the path toward freedom from inherited bondages and into your destiny in Him!

4. Pursue demonic deliverance. Once a stronghold is established, it gives a demon the right to be protected in a bloodline. The Lord is restoring a mantle of deliverance to the Church. Many wonderful books have been written on the subject of demonic deliverance. Few churches, however, are practicing the principles Jesus spent so much time teaching to His disciples on casting out demons. I see a resurgence of this in the future. WE are entering into an incredible time of harvest. And harvest releases God's purpose of redemption and salvation on earth. As we exercise the power of God to become the sons and daughters of God, we will be delivering many into the Kingdom. As we move into the call of Jesus to His disciples to cast out demons, iniquitous patterns that have had rights on the earth will begin to turn, and we will possess our full inheritance.

Notes
1. Cindy Jacobs, *The Voice of God* (Ventura, Calif.: Regal Books, 1995), p. 64.
2. Ibid., pp. 63-64.
3. Buroton Scott Easton, "Naked; Nakedness," *International Standard Bible Encyclopedia* (Electronic Database, 1996 by Biblesoft).
4. Taken from Cindy Jacobs, "Strategies for Spiritual Warfare" tape series 2, Generals of Intercession, P.O. Box 49788, Colorado Springs, CO 80949.
5. Noel and Phyl Gibson, *Evicting Demonic Intruders* (Chichester, England: New Wine Press, 1993), pp. 112-113.
6. Evan Thomas, "The Camelot Curse," *Newsweek*, January 12, 1998, p. 25.
7. Ibid., p. 28.
8. John Eckhardt, *Identifying and Breaking Curses* (Chicago, Ill.: Crusaders Ministries, 1995), p. 1.
9. Ibid., p. 10
10. Charles H. Kraft, *Defeating Dark Angels* (Ann Arbor, Mich.: Servant Publications, 1992), p. 76.
11. Ed Silvoso, *That None Should Perish* (Ventura, Calif.: Regal Books, 1994), p. 231.
12. Francis Frangipane, *The Three Battlegrounds* (Cedar Rapids, Iowa: Arrow Publications, 1989), p. 29.
13. George Howe Colt, "Were You Born That Way?" *Life* (April 1998): 48.
14. Ibid., p. 40.
15. Donovan Webster, "Killer Instinct," *Men's Health* (October 1998): 72.
16. Ibid.
17. Ibid.
18. Noel and Phyl Gibson, *Evicting Demonic Intruders*, pp. 115-119.

NINE

POSSESSING YOUR INHERITANCE

"On the day that I cleanse you from all your iniquities, I will also enable you to dwell in the cities, and the ruins shall be rebuilt. Then the nations which are left all around you shall know that I, the Lord, have rebuilt the ruined places and planted what was desolate. I, the Lord, have spoken it, and I will do it."

—EZEKIEL 36:33,36

We have spent the last two chapters looking at sin issues because without understanding and dealing with these issues, we could not possibly possess all the inheritance the Lord has for us. But sin is not the only thing that keeps us from possessing what God intended.

WHAT PREVENTS US FROM POSSESSING OUR INHERITANCE

Many issues can block the flow of God's blessing in our lives. And though the following list is not comprehensive, it provides several possibilities to consider as you begin to reestablish your Kingdom portion.

1. Ignorance. Often we Christians simply do not know that God has an inheritance for us to possess. We may not understand issues of covenant or the process of spiritual life. If you have understood the principles outlined in this book, this should no longer be an issue for you.

Another aspect of ignorance deals with the revelation the Holy Spirit is bringing in this present season. The enemy longs to capture us in yesterday. If we become so attached to what the Holy Spirit was revealing yesterday that we cannot move forward, then we are in danger of coming under a religious spirit and missing revelation for the present day. The Holy Spirit brings revelation to us in order to give us the wisdom to dismantle the enemy's authority upon the earth. Therefore, if we resist the spirit of truth, which enables us to have fresh power against Satan, we fall into the enemy's trap.

2. Poverty mentality. A poverty mentality keeps us from entering our full potential. Those bound by expectations of poverty never look beyond the narrow scope of the immediate lack in order to find God's rich promises for the future. If we expect to live in poverty, whether physically or spiritually, we will not be disappointed. Poverty says, "God is not capable!" The poverty mentality is not just linked with possessions, but with every issue of supply in our lives, including such things as relationships to God and to one another.

"There is one who scatters, yet increases more; and there is one who withholds more than is right, but it leads to poverty" (Prov. 11:24). If we have a poverty mentality, we tend to resist giving because there may not be enough left over. However, the Word of God says that a mind-set like

that will actually lead to poverty. We must get right in our giving if we are to break out of poverty!

Another issue of poverty is found in Proverbs 21:5, which says, *"The plans of the diligent lead surely to plenty, but those of everyone who is hasty, surely to poverty."* You must learn to wait upon the Lord! To wait means to see the door of opportunity opened to you. If you become hasty and get out of God's timing, you miss your door of opportunity and you are held in poverty.

3. False humility. This differs a little from the poverty mentality. False humility will cause us to say, "I know God has more, but I just don't deserve it." Not one of us deserves all that God has given us. We have all fallen short. But out of His grace and love for us, and because He has a covenant with us, the Lord offers us life abundantly—no matter what we have come out of.

False humility negates confidence and boldness. Confidence and boldness are linked with faith and belief in the gospel of the Lord Jesus Christ. The Early Church was a bold church. False humility is nothing but pride in disguise. It is also linked with a religious spirit that can hold us in undue shame (back to the "I don't deserve it" mentality). Romans 1:16 tells us not be *"ashamed of the gospel of Christ, for it is the power of God to salvation."*

4. Laziness. Though we may not feel that we don't deserve it, some of us just may not want to deal with the responsibility of inheritance. Luke 12:48 says that to whom much is given, much shall be required. We do not possess our inheritance just for our own benefit. As we come into our full covenant with God, He will ask us to use our resulting inheritance to advance His covenant with the earth. Just as in the parable of the talents that Jesus gave in Matthew 25, we are expected to take that which God has given us and expand His kingdom with it.

In Proverbs 15:19 we read that the way of the lazy man is like a hedge of thorns. And Proverbs 22:5 says that thorns and snares are in the way of the perverse. Laziness is linked with perversity and fear. Proverbs 20:13 says, *"Do not love sleep, lest you come to poverty;*

open your eyes, and you will be satisfied with bread." If we do not resist and break free from laziness, it will lead to poverty. If we break free from this spirit, we will begin to see a new level of supply.

5. Fear. Some people do not want to take a risk that may be required in order to possess their inheritance. Earlier in the book I mentioned an example of a couple who, after a miscarriage, are so devastated by the experience that they will not try for more children simply because of the fear of the same thing happening again. Fear can be a gripping and immobilizing force that keeps us from even trying to reach beyond our present circumstances into a future that is unknown. Ask God to break the back of any fear that immobilizes you.

6. Presumption. Satan would love to capture us in one of two ways: either through unbelief or presumption. Many fall into the latter snare by presuming to know what God has for them and how He wants to accomplish His purposes. No one can know exactly what God has in store for them. People who have received prophetic words often begin to work on making the prophecy come to pass, only to be terribly disappointed.

Even if we know in general where the Lord wants to take us, we must allow Him to set our path to get there. Furthermore, we must be prepared that our "there" may not look like we imagined. God's ways are far above ours. And His plan of redemption and inheritance in our lives is far more complete and fulfilling than any plan we might craft on our own.

7. Past woundings. Just as fear can immobilize us, so can past woundings. If we feel we have been treated unjustly, we may not be able to trust God or others enough to stay in our covenant place. We must come to a place of forgiveness and then allow God to heal and soothe those places where we have been too wounded to move forward. If we do not, we will never possess our inheritance.

8. Rebellion/authority problems. We cannot secure our inheritance until our authority structures are in place. That means that God is on the throne of our lives and that we submit not only to Him but also to those who are in authority over us here on earth.

If we have a problem with rebellion and with submitting to biblical authority structures, we must ask the Lord to reveal the root of the problem so we can rid ourselves of it. God cannot lead us into our inheritance if we refuse to follow!

WHAT IS YOUR PORTION?

"O Lord, You are the portion of my inheritance and my cup; You maintain my lot" (Ps. 16:5).

The greatest portion that we as Christians have is, of course, God. In this psalm, we see that David chose God to be his portion. From that choice, God increased and expanded him to Israel's great King David.

The Word of God also talks about portion and inheritance not only in a spiritual sense, but in a physical sense as well. If we, like David, seek God first, He will give us all things (see Matt. 6:33). That means material things as well as spiritual blessings. So many Christians have a poverty mind-set that says God is enough. It is true that God is enough—until He says, "I have set aside that 400 acres for you and My kingdom purposes." Then we have a choice. If we choose to continue saying that God is enough and that we do not need that 400 acres, then we are in disobedience to Him. We will not be in our covenant place with God because we have not taken dominion over what He has set aside for us.

This mind-set of taking dominion over our portion differs from a "prosperity theology" mind-set in that we are not seeking after material things purely for the sake of having them. We are asking God what portion He has already chosen for us and are asking Him to show us the strategy to possess that portion. We do not decide to go out and get 400 acres because we think we ought to have it. Instead, we wait on the Lord for His direction.

By waiting on Him to show us our portion, we accomplish two important things. First, we do not fall into presumption. We don't assume that every piece of 400-acre property that looks desirable is ours and start marching around it, claiming it for ourselves. If God wants us to possess 400 acres, He will show us where, when and how. Furthermore, He will begin to reveal the reason why we are to have that land. God does not increase us just so that we have an impressive portfolio. God increases us for His purposes as well. Of course, He does intend for us to enjoy our inheritance, but He does not intend for us to miss the full purposes He has for our inheritance.

WHEN GOD SPEAKS A PROMISE TO US, WITHIN THAT PROMISE IS ALREADY THE STRATEGY TO OVERTHROW THE DEVIL AND HIS SCHEMES TO BLOCK OUR INHERITANCE.

The second thing we accomplish by waiting on the Lord is that we shut the door on Satan's plan to keep us from what God has ordained—be it through poverty or through presumption. When God speaks a promise to us, within that promise is already the strategy to overthrow the devil and his schemes to block our inheritance. As we wait on the Lord, He will reveal more and more of that strategy to us through prayer.

OUR ABIDING PLACE

To begin securing our portion, we must first understand what and where our abiding place is. There are two facets to being "in the right place at the right time" in order to possess all that God has for us.

1. Spiritual. The first facet is, of course, our spiritual abiding place with the Lord. That is our place of covenant with Him. One of the most beautiful passages in the Bible dealing with our abiding place with the Lord is Psalm 91:

He who dwells in the secret place of the Most High shall abide under the shadow of the Almighty.

I will say of the Lord, "He is my refuge and my fortress; my God, in Him I will trust."

Surely He shall deliver you from the snare of the fowler and from the perilous pestilence.

He shall cover you with His feathers, and under His wings you shall take refuge; His truth shall be your shield and buckler.

You shall not be afraid of the terror by night, nor of the arrow that flies by day,

Nor of the pestilence that walks in darkness, nor of the destruction that lays waste at noonday.

A thousand may fall at your side, and ten thousand at your right hand; but it shall not come near you.

Only with your eyes shall you look, and see the reward of the wicked.

Because you have made the Lord, who is my refuge, even the Most High, your dwelling place,

No evil shall befall you, nor shall any plague come near your dwelling;

For He shall give His angels charge over you, to keep you in all your ways.

In their hands they shall bear you up, lest you dash your foot against a stone.

You shall tread upon the lion and the cobra, the young lion and the serpent you shall trample underfoot.

"Because he has set his love upon Me, therefore I will deliver him; I will set him on high, because he has known My name.

He shall call upon Me, and I will answer him; I will be with him in trouble; I will deliver him and honor him.

With long life I will satisfy him, and show him My salvation."

This psalm is rich with promises for those who *"dwell in the secret place of the Most High."* It not only speaks of the unfailing protection we enjoy from the enemy of our souls, but it also speaks of our authority to tread upon the enemy, angels keeping charge over us, deliverance, honor, a long and satisfying life and salvation. These are all promises of the covenant we have with God when we remain in the abiding place of intimate relationship with Him. Remembering that the greatest part of our inheritance is God Himself, we must take this place of intimacy seriously if we are to fully possess our portion.

2. Physical. There is, however, a second facet to our abiding place that is perhaps less understood, and that is our physical abiding place—where we live and why we live there. Nowhere in the Word of God do we see the Lord separate our spiritual abiding place from our physical abiding place. Places are very important to God. He strategically puts us where we are to live in order to not only possess our own inheritance, but to serve His kingdom.

We talked earlier about David and how he chose God to be his portion in Psalm 16. However, the Psalm goes on to describe the physical abiding place that was part of David's inheritance. Bob Beckett's book *Commitment to Conquer* offers some of the best teaching I have read about why our physical abiding place is so important to God. The following is some of what he has to say with regard to Psalm 16:

> O Lord, You are the portion of my inheritance and my cup; You maintain my lot. The lines have fallen to me in pleasant places; yes, I have a good inheritance. (vv. 5-6)
>
> According to *Strong's Concordance*, the word *lot* in this passage means destiny, portion or land fallen to a person by inheritance....The word *lines* means a measuring line or portion given, again referring to inheritance....If we include the meanings of *lot* and *lines*, Psalm 16:5,6 says that the Lord maintains our lot—the destiny, portion or land fallen to us by inheritance; and that the lines—the measuring or portion given to us by inheritance—have fallen in pleasant places.

God has measured out and given to us some territory for which He will hold us responsible. Just as He gave the Promised Land to the children of Israel, so He gives us a portion of land for which we will someday answer. This part of our inheritance is also echoed in Jeremiah 32:41: "And I will assuredly *plant* them in this land" (italics added).

This does not mean every believer in Jesus Christ is guaranteed to hold the deed to a piece of property. It does mean we are placed strategically within a community or territory for the purposes of God. This is our assigned sphere of influence. Where God has planted us in the land is the place we will have the greatest impact for His Kingdom.[1]

Beckett goes on with this exhortation:

Even if there is somewhere else you long to be, ask yourself two questions:

Who put you where you are?

Why are you there?

There can be only two answers to these questions: obedience or rebellion. You are in a place either because God put you there or because you put yourself there....

If you are where you are out of rebellion, I have a word for you: Move, as fast as you can! Find out where God wants you and get there. Even if it feels as if you are being led out of Jerusalem into Babylon, remember that the Lord sees far beyond what you or I can see in our lives. Obedience to God always bring ultimate peace.

If you know God has placed you where you are, even if it seems like Babylon, I have a word for you: Stay there as long as God asks.[2]

Our covenantal blessings and our inheritance will never be fully realized without being where God calls us to be. Many Christians don't understand the principle of being in the abiding place so they become frustrated when they don't see God work in their lives. But we must seek Him spiritually *and* establish ourselves in the land that He has given to us before we can be fully in the abiding place He has for us. Even the Israelites who were exiles in a foreign land were commanded by God to seek the welfare of the cities to which they were deported (see Jer. 29:7). Acts 17:26 says that He predetermines the place where you are to seek Him. In that predetermined physical place, you will begin to find Him spiritually and begin to gain the strategy necessary to secure your portion.

SECURING YOUR PORTION

"I will fasten him as a peg in a secure place" (Isa. 22:23).

To secure means to put beyond the hazard of losing. It means to bring something to a place of hope or safety; to be fastened, planted and established. When we secure something, we have removed it from exposure to danger. Secure also means to have a feeling of trust or confidence. When we don't have confidence, we have lost a place of security within us. But God longs to fasten us in a secure place.

As Matthew 6:19 reminds us, our security does not come from treasures stored up for ourselves here on earth where moth and rust destroy and thieves break in and steal—or where the stock market can crash. Our security must be firmly fastened in God. When we have that in order, then we can secure our inheritance. That does not mean that we will never experience any loss (as we discussed at length in chapter 3). But it does mean that anything we have has been given to us by God, and as long as we position ourselves correctly in the Lord, the inheritance God has for us is securely fastened in Him.

PRAYER, PRAYER, PRAYER!

How can we be sure that we remain in our secure abiding place with the Lord? The answer is prayer—active intercessory prayer. In the

Hebrew, the word for intercessory prayer is *paga*. While this is a rich word with many meanings, there are four specific meanings to this word that we must understand if we are to secure our inheritance[3]:

1. **Meeting.** When we *paga*, we are actually meeting. We are meeting with God in an intimate place so we can present ourselves to Him and then inquire of Him what path He would have us walk. But often this place of meeting is twofold. Having met with God and gained strategy from Him, we are often required to confront the powers that have torn down or weakened our inheritance. We meet the enemy.

Many people are willing to meet God in an intimate place, but do not secure their inheritance because they are unwilling to turn and meet the enemy who is holding back what is theirs. It takes both. It is true that we go from glory to glory to glory, not from warfare to warfare to warfare. But, as we're going from glory to glory to glory, we must confront the enemy who will attempt to keep us from establishing ourselves in our new place of glory—our abiding place. And since our inheritance is secure when we are in our proper abiding place, it behooves us to do whatever warfare is necessary to evict the enemy from our abiding place.

Therefore, when we *paga*, we are not only meeting with God, but we are also meeting the enemy head-on. In his insightful book *Intercessory Prayer*, Dutch Sheets describes this definition of *paga* in the following way:

> I am saying, however, that the word for "meet" is our Hebrew word translated "intercession," *paga*. Other Hebrew words could have been used, but this one was chosen partly because it often has a very violent connotation. In fact, *paga* is frequently a battlefield term (for examples see: Judges 8:21; 15:12; 1 Sam. 22:17,18; 2 Sam. 1:15; 1 Kings 2:25-46).
>
> Intercession can be violent!
>
> *Meetings* can be unpleasant! Some can be downright ugly!
>
> Such as the one Satan had with Jesus at Calvary when

Christ interceded for us....Satan's worst nightmare came
true when with 4,000 years of pent-up fury, Jesus *met* him
at Calvary....At the moment of what Satan thought was his
greatest triumph, he and all his forces heard the most terri-
fying sound they had ever heard, God's laugh of derision!
(see Ps. 2:4).[4]

This illustration from Sheets is a picture of Christ *paga*-ing in
order to possess our greatest inheritance—that of salvation. Another
example is when the children of Israel reached the Promised Land,
which was their new abiding place, and met the enemy in the form
of giants inhabiting the land. The giants needed to be driven out so
the Israelites could possess their inheritance. They were *paga*-ing the
enemy. To secure that which God longs for us to secure, we must be
willing to face our spiritual enemies just as the Israelites faced their
physical enemies.

2. To strike down. It is not enough to meet the enemy. We must
also strike the enemy down through active warfare intercession.
Dutch Sheets describes it this way:

Although imbalances occur, nonetheless, it is impossible to
separate the word intercession, *paga*, from warfare....I tell you
emphatically, *violence and war are rooted in the very meaning of the
word*. It is translated in various ways when speaking of warfare: "attack," "fall upon," "strike down," "impinge" as well as
others (see Judg. 8:21; 1 Sam. 22:11-19; 2 Sam. 1:11-16: The
essence is the same in all of them—people in battle attacking
one another). Hear me clearly: *Paga* involves warfare![5]

Through intercession we are able to strike down that which is
keeping us from our inheritance. Once we *paga*, strike down, there
is a bruising, a shattering of the enemy that occurs. When we wield
the sword of the Spirit, we have the authority to strike down that
which is holding back our inheritance.

3. To strike the mark. In order to strike down the enemy effectively, we must know exactly what we are striking at. Bob Beckett calls this "smart bomb" praying. He describes it in the following words:

> I went to the Lord earnestly seeking answers. And gradually He began to show me what our problem was. Although we had been interceding faithfully, our intercession had not been persistently accurate. We had simply sprayed prayers here and there, hoping they would hit a target....
>
> The Gulf War offered a model. The bombs of the Allied forces knew their exact targets and, for the most part, destroyed specific buildings or sites—nothing more, nothing less....That, I thought, is how our intercession should be. We knew the value of prayer. We knew how to bind demonic forces. We were willing to put in the time and energy. We did not have enough understanding, however, of what our enemy was doing to hold (us) in bondage. We did not know how to aim our prayers in such a way as to destroy Satan's strongholds.[6]

Unfortunately, many times our prayers do not strike the mark. Therefore, we are not casting down that which is holding back our full portion. As we meet with the Lord and earnestly seek Him for the keys to striking the mark, He will show us where to aim our prayers in order to hit the mark and strike down whatever enemy is attempting to keep us from securing our inheritance.

4. Set your boundaries. Another meaning of *paga* is to set boundaries (as used in Josh. 16:7; 19:11,22,26,27,34). Boundaries are the fixed limit or extent of your authority. We must allow God to set the boundaries of our inheritance. It is within those boundaries that we are in our secure place and that we have the authority to war. We do not have the authority to war outside of those boundaries. If we do, we will fall into presumption and take on the enemy in wars that are too great for us, because God has not assigned them to us. Therefore, if we try *paga*-ing outside of the limit God has set for us, we will not be able to strike down the enemy. In fact, we are in great danger of being struck down.

Simply put, when you cross over the boundary set for you by God, you step out of His grace. Some people have even been killed prematurely by doing so. Yet I have found that due to our innate rebellious nature, we often detest boundaries because they enclose and restrict us. But God can't bring us to a true place of stewardship until He knows that He can trust us to remain within the boundaries He has set for us. Therefore, if you are tempted to extend yourself beyond those boundaries, you must deal with your rebellious nature. Once you have learned to live within God's limits, however, He will then be able to trust you with an extended boundary.

A SEASON OF INHERITANCE

Ecclesiastes 3 reminds us that for everything there is a season and a time for every purpose under heaven. For the children of Israel, God ordained that every 50 years was to be a Jubilee Year. Jubilee signified a return of one's possessions. Not only were debts released from prior years, but individuals also had the right to regain their inheritance. Properties were to be returned to the original owners or their heirs, and bountiful provision was made.

In his excellent book *In That Day*, Rabbi David Levine spells out two of the promises of Jubilee:

> *First, the triple harvest is promised.*...As I contemplate this, I realize that God desires to offer His substantial provision even *before* the need is present. This is one of the miracles of God's provision....However it might be labeled, I have seen that need alone does not always stir God to move. However, when He shows us His ways and we walk along His path no matter how narrow it might get, we find that the vision He gives us is accompanied by His provision.

*Second is the promise that inhabitants of Israel will be restored to their inheritance and possessions....*While this was to apply to farm land only, not to the land and houses within walled cities, it suggests to us that God is concerned that we receive our inheritance and that anything lost be returned.[7]

Isaiah 61 is thought by many scholars to proclaim a final end-times Jubilee "year" of God's favor (see v. 2). As believers, we see this promise fulfilled in Christ (see Luke 4:18-21). But there are seasons in our lives that are ordained by God which can be thought of as modern Jubilees. During those times God's favor does rest upon us. In a sense, as children of God, we continually walk in favor with Him in that we always have access to the throne of God through Christ. Favor is like grace. But it differs in that it is linked with obedience, and obedience is linked with holiness. We are more likely to be living under God's favor as we live lives that are acceptable to Him.

But there are special, appointed times when we walk in a greater measure of favor. It may be when our children are born, or when we marry God's chosen mate, or any number of similar blessed times. It is then that we have entered a favorable year or season of the Lord. In fact, all of Isaiah 61 speaks of many aspects of restoration, such as beauty for ashes, the oil of joy for mourning, the garment of praise for the spirit of heaviness, healing for the brokenhearted, liberty for the captives, sight for the blind, double honor for shame and so forth.

It is in this favorable year, in a year of Jubilee, that we have access to secure our inheritance. And to secure our inheritance, we must have favor. But the enemy does not like favor because he knows that once the glory of God and the favor of God rest upon us, he will be seen for who he is. So as we enter into a favorable season, our warfare is likely to increase. But the Lord's provision for that warfare is already at our disposal, and as we secure our victory, we secure our inheritance.

LESSONS FROM JOSEPH

The story of Joseph is an outstanding biblical example of complete restoration. Throughout his life Joseph experienced seasons of loss and seasons of favor. When his full restoration came, however, his own inheritance was restored, his family's inheritance was secured, and a nation was saved from famine!

JOSEPH FAVORED

The story of Joseph begins in Genesis 37. Scripture tells us that Joseph was a faithful son. His father, Jacob, loved him more than his brothers and to demonstrate that love gave him a coat of many colors. That coat represented favor and the double-portion anointing that came along with that favor.

God longs to put a mantle of favor on us just as Jacob gave to Joseph. Favor gives us access to doors that would not be open to us otherwise. Yet like Joseph, we must learn how to wear favor as we do a special garment and protect it from the enemy.

We all wear some type of figurative garment, but not all garments we wear represent the favor of God. Many times our garments are made up of past losses that have embedded themselves in our emotions and become a part of our lives. Our garments may drip with hope deferred that has caused sickness of heart. Our garments may be made up of past reproaches. Favor is the opposite of reproach. As we cast off the garment of reproach, we can put on God's garment of favor.

JOSEPH BETRAYED

Just because we wear a garment of favor does not mean that the enemy cannot attack us. Joseph's brothers knew the coat meant that Joseph had received the best of the inheritance. They knew that if they received one portion, Joseph would receive two. Jealousy overtook them. So when Joseph's brothers saw his garment of favor, they became so enraged that they literally tore it from him, threw blood all over it, and, leaving Joseph for dead, took the coat of favor back to his father and basically said, "Here's the favor you gave your son." Joseph was betrayed and his favor was stripped from him.

Betrayals come against us to remove the favor of God and are linked with covenant breaking. Divorce is one example of this. Betrayal is one of the most painful things we may have to deal with; it was for Jesus, too. It was one of the things He agonized through as He interceded before His death. He knew the betrayal that was ahead of Him.

Joseph's betrayal made him a slave. But even though he was betrayed, we see in Genesis 39:2 that the Lord was with him and caused him to prosper. Verse 4 says, *"So Joseph found favor in his [master's] sight, and served him. Then [the master] made [Joseph] overseer of his house, and all that he had he put under his authority."* Because Joseph was faithful even in the midst of his betrayal, he suddenly found new favor resting upon him once again. Betrayal was not the end. Have any past betrayals withheld the favor of God from resting upon you?

JOSEPH ACCUSED

But now his master's wife longed for the favor of Joseph for herself. We pick up the story in Genesis 39:11-14: *"But it happened about this time, when Joseph went into the house to do his work, and none of the men of the house was inside, that she caught him by his garment, saying, 'Lie with me.' But he left his garment in her hand, and fled and ran outside. And so it was, when she saw that he had left his garment in her hand and fled outside, that she called to the men of her house and spoke to them."*

His master's wife began to wrongly accuse Joseph by using the garment she tore from his body as false evidence. Joseph had finally been reclothed with favor only to find himself suddenly naked again. Joseph had a hard time keeping his clothes on! Just like the master's wife, our enemy wants to strip our favor and keep us in shame. Ask the Lord if the false accusations that have come against you have prevented the favor of God from rising upon you.

Here was Joseph in shame after being falsely accused and now he lands in prison. But as the story progresses, we see that Joseph finds favor once again—this time in the sight of the prison keeper (see Gen. 39:21). His favor was back on him, even in prison. In everything that he did, the Lord made him prosper. Just like Joseph, you and I can prosper in any circumstance—even in prison!

JOSEPH FORGOTTEN AND ABANDONED

As Joseph's life moves on, we see that he used the gifts God had given him, both to prosper and to help others in the prison. In Genesis 40, Joseph is called upon to interpret dreams, which he does with great accuracy. His interpretation of the chief butler's dream was that he would be released from prison and restored into favor in Pharaoh's house. Joseph asks the chief butler to remember him to Pharaoh, but the butler forgets him and leaves him in prison for two more years.

IF THE POWER OF REJECTION CAN CONVINCE US THAT NO ONE KNOWS OUR GIFTINGS OR THAT WE HAVE A DESTINY ON THIS EARTH, THE ENEMY WILL TOTALLY CAPTURE US.

The power of rejection and abandonment works to make us think that we are totally forgotten and God does not know where we are. If that power can convince us that no one knows our giftings or knows where we are or that we have a destiny on this earth, the enemy will totally capture us.

My wife, Pam, learned this lesson as we went through one of the hardest seasons we have ever experienced in our 25 years of marriage. I have already told the story of how the Lord healed Pam from barrenness. What I didn't tell is that before Pam received her healing, she had confidence that God would heal her at the appropriate time, because in 1980 He had told her that she would give birth to twins. And in order to have those twins, she would need to be healed. So when Pam was pregnant for the third time, we learned that she was indeed going to have twins. She carried those babies to full term, but shortly after birth, they both died. It was devastating. Not only did we have to deal with the loss of two children, but also the loss of God's promise being fulfilled as we had anticipated.

The next months were very hard. One day Pam confessed to me that she saw nothing but death in our house. The goldfish had died and her garden had died. Each death accentuated the loss of our children. She was in a hard place. Finally she cried out to God and asked Him to show her that He knew how hard things were and that He had not completely forgotten her in her grief.

Soon after that, as we were driving back home from a trip, Pam reminded me that the only thing she had from her first 12 years of life before her father committed suicide was a packet of pictures. Even though her family had been destroyed, her childhood was still her childhood and those pictures meant a great deal to her. But she said she really hadn't remembered seeing those pictures since I had graduated from college 14 years prior. She spent a solid week scouring the house for that only memento of her early childhood.

When we arrived home from our trip, we immediately went to pick up the mail and found a plain brown paper envelope. Much to our shock the envelope contained Pam's pictures and a letter. The letter read, "Evidently these pictures are yours. I bought a used truck that apparently belonged to you in your college days. I was cleaning out the truck a month ago and found this packet of pictures. With the pictures was a blank check that had the name 'Charles Pierce, 305 Ball Street, College Station, Texas.' (We had since lived in Houston for 12 years and had moved from there to Denton, Texas.) I called a Charles Pierce in College Station who knew nothing about this, so I called the former student association and traced your habitation through these last years. I am now return-ing these pictures to you."

Suddenly, the Spirit of God fell upon our home, and the Lord said to Pam, "I know where you are, and I can find you anytime. I have not forgotten you. I know everything about you. I know your past, and I know your future. I know what you are going through, and I know how you are feeling. I have found you this day. Rejoice in Me."

Have your past rejections and abandonments kept God's favor from resting upon you?

JOSEPH'S INHERITANCE SECURED

Even though Joseph felt forgotten and abandoned in the prison, God knew where he was. And God began to move on Pharaoh. God will move on even the highest officials to see His covenant purposes secured. Because Joseph had been faithful in prison and had used his gift to interpret dreams, the Lord exalted him when the time was right. Even in the toughest circumstances, God can move on anybody on your behalf if you will submit yourself to Him. He loves you so much that He will do whatever is necessary to see you accomplish your role upon this earth. If you will let your gifts work when you are in captivity and in hard circumstances, God will exalt those gifts at the right time into their proper place.

As God exalted Joseph to Pharaoh, we see that once again Joseph changes his clothes (see Gen. 41:14) and a new favor is placed upon him. God then gave Joseph a strategy to save the entire nation from famine. He was now entering into his destiny. But the real issue for Joseph was not that God took care of Egypt in the famine. The real issue was that God sovereignly positioned Joseph to see that the inheritance God had for him and his family was firmly secured. In that same way, God will position whatever is necessary to cause the giftings He has deposited in you to come to their fullness. He has not forgotten you. He will do what is necessary to see you accomplish what He has called you to accomplish.

There is one more lesson on securing inheritance to be learned from Joseph, and that is the lesson of forgiveness. Once Joseph revealed himself to his brothers, they were fearful and dismayed, because Joseph had tremendous power to retaliate for their betrayal. But instead Joseph chose to forgive. That one action brought restoration to his whole family that would birth the nation of Israel and would set in motion God's covenant plan for His chosen people.

In order to keep our garment of favor from being snatched away, we must have a supernatural ability to forgive. We must release our perpetrators. Forgiveness produces both grace and favor, and keeps us clothed in the coat of many colors the Lord has fashioned for us.

Stop! Review your life. Outline your testimony. Spend some time with God and let His favor rest upon you new and afresh.

RUTH: AN INHERITANCE RESTORED

The account of Ruth is one of my favorite stories in the Bible. Here was a woman with no hope for any meaningful future. Yet because of her obedience to a covenant, her life was released into a fullness of joy. She was restored beyond anything she could have imagined or hoped for.

The story of Ruth has four essential elements: Naomi, Boaz, Ruth and the city of Bethlehem. The story opens with Naomi, whose family had great wealth and inheritance, living in Bethlehem. But famine began to overtake the city of Bethlehem. Not knowing what to do, the whole family left that area, left their inheritance behind and went to Moab. Naomi's two sons married in the new land and later died there. Naomi's husband also died there. Famine, death and desolation caused all hope for inheritance to be lost. Naomi had absolutely nothing left but two daughters-in-law, one of whom was Ruth.

Naomi, whose name meant pleasant, had nothing in her heart but bitterness. She even declared that she was to be called "bitter." The enemy can so assault us in our lives that the very opposite of what God intends for us becomes our identity. For Naomi that meant that her pleasantness had turned to bitterness. Yet, she remembered that the inheritance her family once had was back in Bethlehem, not in Moab, so she decided to go back.

Naomi brought her two daughters-in-law together and told them that she could not promise them a better life in Bethlehem because when she left, it was in desolation. One daughter-in-law decided to stay in Moab. God has places of choice for us. When we get to a key deciding place in our lives, we find a biblical principle at work: God always gives us the opportunity to either go all the way or to turn around and go back.

But Ruth committed to go with Naomi. She said, *"I will* go and *I will* die, if necessary" (see Ruth 1:16,17). "I will" is one of the most powerful phrases in the Bible. Ruth made covenant with Naomi when she said, "I will." Ruth was committed to fight by Naomi's side in spite of any enemies or difficulties that might come their way. Most of us really do not fully understand the true power of covenant to affect not only ourselves but also a territory. This covenant stirred things up in Bethlehem. Two widows entering a city was hardly cause for celebration. Yet the Bible says that when Ruth and Naomi came through the gates of Bethlehem, all the city was excited (see v. 19).

When they arrived back in Bethlehem, all they had was Ruth's covenant with Naomi and a long-lost inheritance that was somehow linked with this city. Ruth served Naomi faithfully. She was a woman of virtue, filled with power because of her commitment. She would glean in the fields, which meant that she would come behind the reapers and pick up the leftover grain in order to make the bread that would sustain them for one more day.

Finally Naomi told Ruth that things had to change. This gleaning wasn't getting them anywhere. So Naomi decided to seek security for Ruth. She wanted to secure Ruth's inheritance. She realized that Boaz was a relative and that there was a spiritual law over the area that provided for a relative to bring them back into their inheritance. Suddenly a light went on in Naomi's mind. God established provision for them in the Levitical law that said they had a right to family inheritance if the relative would become their kinsman redeemer.

So, Naomi laid out a plan for Ruth to secure her inheritance. This is what she told her to do:

1. Wash yourself. Ruth had been gleaning in the fields. She was tired and smelled. Naomi knew they were not going to come into an inheritance with the way Ruth looked. So Ruth brought the water and began to wash herself. Today the Lord is sweeping across His Body with cleansing revelation. We have worked hard. We have toiled in the fields and God says, "Stop. Wash yourself. Let the Word of God flow over you. Take a rest. Soak for a little while and allow the cleansing to refresh and renew."

2. Anoint yourself. To anoint means to be smeared with fragrant oil. Ruth needed a new fragrance for the new season. Isaiah 61 speaks of the oil of joy that replaces the mourning in our souls. This is also a part of Jubilee. Ruth had not been in a season of joy. Rather, she had been in widowhood. But in order to move into her season of inheritance, she needed a new anointing of oil that would emit a pleasant fragrance. As you move into your season of inheritance, allow the Holy Spirit to cover you with a new anointing. Allow the oil of joy to replace the unpleasant odor of mourning in your life.

3. Put on your best garment. The garment that Ruth had been wearing to work in the field was inappropriate. Remember Ruth was still in her widow's garment. In order to secure her future, the widowhood that was dressed around her had to come off. The grief that she had been wearing was no good for the next place. It would not draw anyone to her. Like Joseph, Ruth needed to put on a new garment to move into her next place. Here is a lesson for us: Take off the grief. We go through hard, hard things. But when God says it's time to change your garments and remove your grief, don't let any self-pity keep that old garment buttoned up on you. Can we draw in the people of the world if we are clothed with grief? No. God is going to have us put on a new garment that will show the world the comfort and encouragement they need. Just as Ruth and

Joseph did, get ready to take off that old garment and put on a whole new mantle.

4. Go to the threshing floor. The threshing floor had a dual purpose in those days. It was where the wheat and the chaff were separated. But it was also a place of feasting. So here Naomi says, "Ruth, I want you to go to the place where the party is being held." As we make ourselves ready, God is preparing a feast for us, and He is preparing us to go to the place where the party is happening.

5. Wait for God's timing. Naomi told Ruth not to enter into the party right away. She was to stand back and wait until all the fun stopped and then come out of the shadows. God is getting us established in our abiding place so we are ready when the time comes. Then Ruth was to go lay down at Boaz's feet, and as she did, there would be a distinct decision made. Can you imagine what Ruth must have been thinking? She was a virtuous woman. And now she was told to lay down at the feet of a man. This was a true test of submission. God is bringing the Body of Christ to His feet, and we are to stay there until we receive the best.

BOAZ SECURES RUTH'S INHERITANCE

Boaz woke from his sleep and saw Ruth lying there. Then Boaz, a beautiful picture of our kinsman redeemer in the Lord Jesus, asked her who she was. Ruth identified herself as a close relative and asked him to draw her in and cover her. Fuchsia Pickett describes Ruth's request this way: "In asking Boaz to cover her, Ruth was declaring, 'I need a redeemer. I am a widow, disgraced, with no inheritance. You can take my shame, my poverty, the bleakness of my future and give me an inheritance. You can totally redeem me, if you will.' "[8]

Boaz then explained to Ruth that there was a relative closer to her than he, and that there was an issue of order that had not been dealt with. When we pull aside, God will show us some key issues of order that we have not seen before. Then Boaz went to see the relative who had first rights to Ruth. Boaz was determined that Ruth's inheritance would be secured one way or another. If we, God's people, will pull aside this day at His feet and submit ourselves to Him and be willing to do whatever He says, He will secure our inheritance one way or another. God is saying, "Come to My feet. You will not lose out. I will see that your inheritance is secured. For you are at a crossroads, but when the day breaks, your inheritance will be there for you one way or another."

Then Boaz stood at the gates of Bethlehem and warred for Ruth before receiving her as his wife. The redemptive plan of God could not be stopped. The seed of inheritance went into Ruth, and she conceived a child. That child was brought to Naomi who was still bitter, yet she began to nourish that child. A life flow began to pour out of Naomi and nourish that seed of her inheritance. The child produced from Ruth's union with Boaz was Obed, King David's grandfather and a direct ancestor to our Lord Jesus. As such, all generations have been blessed by the restoration of Naomi's inheritance, Ruth's covenant alliance, and Boaz's obedience in the gates of Bethlehem.

Boaz means "God is my strength." God can be your strength to restore everything you have lost. God is about to draw us under His wing. As we understand His covenant with us, we will have the ability to do the strange things He requires of us—then He will draw us near and redeem us fully. Be ready, for we are changing seasons. And because of our obedience, God has a plan to bring out the glory of our latter days in a much greater proportion than you or I had in the beginning!

He has a plan to see that we possess and secure our inheritance. The following are some keys to help you advance into your future.

1. Know that you have a future. The enemy longs to convince us that we have no future, or that one mistake will cause all the plans ahead to go awry. Regardless of your circumstances, you have a latter end. Jeremiah prophesied to many individuals as they approached their captivity. He told them to settle down in Babylon—build, plant gardens, and continue the propagation of the generations by giving their sons and daughters in marriage. Often when we go through a time of discipline, we begin to feel abandoned. Condemnation becomes a way of life. We do not stop to think that the Lord is taking us through this season so we can be restored and eventually secure what He has for us further along our paths. He knows when our present direction will stop the ultimate flow of His blessings. That was the issue God was communicating through Jeremiah in 29:11: *"For I know the thoughts and plans that I have for you, says the Lord, thoughts and plans for welfare and peace and not for evil, to give you hope in your final outcome—to give you a future hope"* (my paraphrase). Commit to the Lord today where you are—new and fresh—and watch your future unfurl before your eyes.

2. Worship to gain revelation. The Lord spoke to me at the beginning of the year and said, "The key for My people this year is to understand worship. If they will understand worship, they will understand faith. If they will activate their faith, they will see the changes that I desire in heaven come to earth." I began to look in the Word and find the first man of faith to be Abel. As he worshiped the way God instructed, he encountered problems from his brother Cain. Worship brings favor. This is a year of favor. Even though Abel was killed because of his worship, his blood or (inheritance of worship) cried from the ground until generations to come would worship the Lord, as He desires. Worship opens up our path into the throne room. From that place we gain our strategy to build what the Lord wants built on earth. In Paul's letter to Ephesus, he prays for them to know the Lord intimately, so they may know the hope of their calling.

3. As the Lord releases His prophetic word and directives to you, embrace and activate them in your life. The Lord began to release the prophetic to earth when He first said, "Let there be light!" This caused the chaos and disorder to take form and new order to begin. Every time God speaks to us, a new order begins. All through the Word, we find instances of how the Lord would speak, either directly or through a prophet, and the strategy for victory or advancement would occur. A great example is 2 Chronicles 20. The prophet speaks to King Jehoshaphat; he embraces the word, and victory occurs. So many times, because we hear the word of the Lord but fail to embrace what God is saying, we encounter desolation or failure. Embrace your revelation today!

4. Frequently review and evaluate your vision. Many hear God but, in the daily warfare and opposition, lose sight of what He said. The vision is clear when you first receive revelation, but grows foggy as the time of fulfillment is prolonged. Without a vision people perish or go backwards. Thus we must disciple and subdue our flesh so our spiritual lives will maintain buoyancy. Write your vision as Habakkuk instructs. Record the flow of decisions you have made, paths you have taken, and consequences for choices since the time the Lord spoke to you. In other words, how did you get to this place? Determine whether you are walking in an overcoming strength or in defeat. Ask the Lord "supply" questions relative to your vision. Ask Him about timing issues. Let Him order your steps to victory.

5. Surround yourself with the right connections and associations. *"Do not let your heart envy sinners, but be zealous for the fear of the Lord all the day; for surely there is a hereafter [future] and your hope will not be cut off"* (Prov. 23:17,18). In this hour, connections are important. Be sure you choose well your associations. Know who labors among you. Key connections form a net that works. Wrong connections thwart or prolong what the Lord has in store for us. Pray this for your children.

6. Be willing to obey, even if the Lord asks you to do something unusual. Jerusalem was being besieged and the Lord was giving a future warning that the present government would be sent into captivity. The entire nation had been led into defilement and judgment because they had entered into idol worship in the House of the Lord. Then the word of the Lord comes to Jeremiah (see Jer. 32:6-9) of his right of redemption and inheritance to buy the field that belonged to his uncle in Anathoth. He made a declaration of the Lord's faithfulness and bought the field. He buried the deed and a copy in the land. However his mind eventually kicked into gear and he began to question the Lord's wisdom. The Lord then asks him, "Is there anything too hard for Me? Can't I cause that which has fallen into ruins to be rebuilt?" The Lord was really saying, "Secure your inheritance now during desolate times and when it is time for Me to flourish this area again, that which you have planted will arise for the next generation." The Lord is getting ready to cause things to sprout. Don't hesitate to do what He asks. Obedience results in God's holy character being seen on earth.

7. Don't let obstacles stop you from reaching your destination. Another instance of exhortation came through the prophet Zechariah. He said to Zerubbabel, *"Who are you, O great mountain? Before Zerubbabel you shall become a plain [a molehill]! And he shall bring forth the capstone with shouts of 'Grace, grace to it!'"* (Zech. 4:7). The Babylonian captivity had ended. The people had almost completed the rebuilding of the city. Now they were rebuilding the Temple. During this rebuilding process, the enemy began to lambaste them with accusations. Ezra 4:4 says, *"Then the peoples around them set out to discourage the people of Judah and make them afraid to go on building"* (NIV). Eventually the rebuilding of the Temple stopped. The Body of Christ is in a "building or rebuilding season." I have sensed discouragement in many individuals. The Lord wants to release a new joy. Joy produces strength. Strength causes us to complete our assignments. In Haggai, we find the prophet prophesying in a similar vain, saying that a shaking would come to break them of discouragement so they could see the glory of the latter house. Let God shake you so you can begin to see your future. The enemy will send anything he can into your path to stop you. He will threaten you with death, send infirmities, stop supply, accuse, etc., etc., etc.! SHOUT GRACE and watch the obstacle fall!

8. Establish the Watchman strategy for your inheritance. The Old Testament discusses three watches; the New Testament discusses four watches. When the Lord created humankind, He called them to "tend" or watch over the garden in which He had placed them. You each have a garden. You each have an inheritance. You each have a future. Be sure that through communion, you gain the plan of victory for the Lord's fullness to be displayed in your garden. To "watch" means to observe or look after. We often fall into presumption, expecting the Lord to accomplish something He has previously spoken when it was conditional upon our obedience. We forget the stewardship principle. We fall into passivity and our gardens become overrun. Our future is then deferred to another generation that will clean the garden and restore the field. Develop your strategy for watching in the days ahead so your inheritance is secured.

Enter into a new dimension of victory this hour. Root all deception and disobedience out of your vision. Homemakers, that may be the placement and training of your children. Business people, that may be the organization the Lord has given you to prosper. Pastors, that may be the city in which the Lord has called you to minister and shepherd His flock. Missionaries, that may be the people group God has called you to. Wherever you are, you have a future and a hope. Find your boundaries and abound. Possess your inheritance!

Notes

1. Bob Beckett, *Commitment to Conquer* (Grand Rapids, Mich.: Chosen Books, 1997), pp. 55-56.
2. Ibid., pp. 65-66.
3. For a more complete study of the word *paga*, I highly recommend Dutch Sheets's book, *Intercessory Prayer* (Ventura, Calif.: Regal Books, 1996).
4. Ibid., p. 55.
5. Ibid., p. 138.
6. Bob Beckett, *Commitment to Conquer*, pp. 32, 34.
7. David Levine, *In That Day* (Lake Mary, Fla.: Creation House, 1998), p. xiv, xv.
8. Fuchsia Pickett, *The Prophetic Romance* (Orlando, Fla.: Creation House, 1996), pp. 9, 108.

INDEX

Live in Victory!

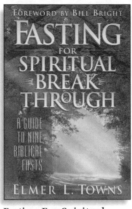

Go and Sin No More
Dr. Michael L. Brown
A Call to Holiness
Hardcover
ISBN 08307.23951

Fasting For Spiritual Breakthrough
Elmer L. Towns
A Guide to Nine Biblical Fasts
Paperback • ISBN 08307.18397
Study Guide
ISBN 08307.18478

Biblical Meditation for Spiritual Breakthrough
Elmer L. Towns
Cultivating a Deeper Relationship with the Lord Through Biblical Meditation
Paperback • ISBN 08307.23609

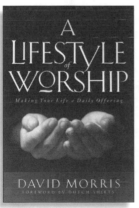

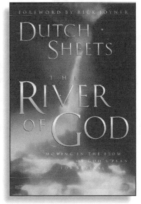

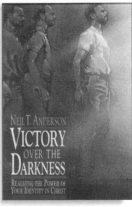

A Lifestyle of Worship
David Morris
Making Your Life a Daily Offering
Paperback • ISBN 08307.21991

The River of God
Dutch Sheets
Moving in the Flow of God's Plan for Revival
Paperback • ISBN 08307.20758

Victory over the Darkness
Neil T. Anderson
Realizing the Power of Your Identity in Christ
Paperback ISBN 08307.13751

Available at your local Christian bookstore.

Regal
FROM GOSPEL LIGHT

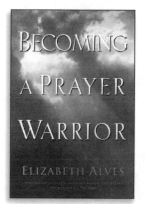

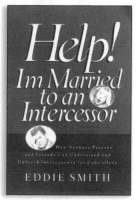
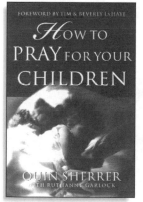
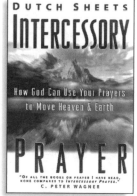
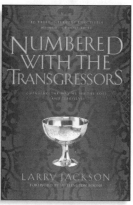